INSIGHT CO

Bahamas

Compact Guide: Bahamas is the ideal quick-reference guide to these paradise islands. It tells you all you need to know about the islands' attractions, from beautiful palm-fringed beaches to the marvels of the coral reefs, candy-colored clapboard houses to carnival and superstition, stories of pirates and shipwrecks to relics of the colonial past.

This is just one title in *Apa Publications'* new series of pocket-sized, easy-to-use guidebooks intended for the independent-minded traveler. *Compact Guides* pride themselves on being up-to-date and authoritative. They are in essence mini travel encyclopedias, designed to be comprehensive yet portable, as well as readable and reliable.

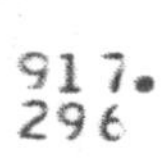

Star Attractions

A quick reference to some of the Bahamas' most popular tourist attractions to help you on your way.

Government House, Nassau p21

Straw Market p22

Dolphin Experience p30

Junkanoo Expo p22

Grand Bahama p27

International Bazaar p29

Spanish Wells, Eleuthera p36

The Abacos p37

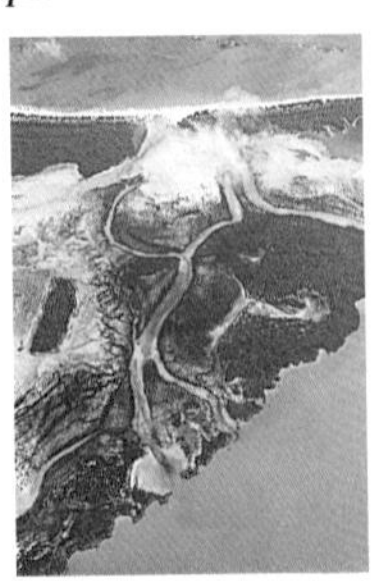

Exuma Cays p42

Andros p49

Lake Windsor p52

Bahamas

Introduction

Places

Culture

Leisure

Practical Information

The Bahamas – Paradise on Earth

The Bahamas may not be able to offer everything your heart desires, but they hold a wealth of priceless treasures which captivate most visitors and leave memories that last a lifetime. There are almost 3,000 islands, if every patch of land that emerges from the sea is counted. About 700 of them can really claim to be islands, and of these, 30 are inhabited. On the Bahamas it is possible to venture into wild, untamed swamps, visit coral reefs, watch dolphins at play, enjoy the sun on a lonely island (probably the closest thing to paradise on earth) and bathe in a sea, which shimmers in tones of blue and green. There are beaches which surfers consider among the best in the world for their exhilarating sport, and others which look as if yours are the first feet to tread on them. And the fish and seafood which comes out of the clear waters will be some of the freshest you have ever tasted.

Opposite: Paradise islands

Clifton Point, New Providence

In the capital, Nassau, you may be pleasantly surprised to find how cosmopolitan and sophisticated life is. Casinos and cabarets to entertain you at night, internationally known names in the shopping streets to tempt you during the day, strains of calypso music wherever you go, and tantalizing aromas to whet your appetite. But to get to know the real Bahamas, you should venture far away from the tourist centres of Nassau and Freeport/Lucaya, at least for a little while and pay the Out Islands a visit. Here the pace of life is unusually relaxing and gentle. You can get to know the friendly Bahamian people at home in their villages, or enjoying themselves at local festivals – something they are very good at. Or if you are not in the mood for company you can enjoy the peace and beauty of the islands undisturbed – solitude is easier to find here than in most parts of the world. Once you have done so, you'll almost certainly want to come back.

Sophisticated airs

Position and size

In geographical terms the Bahamas are considered Caribbean islands but in fact, the archipelago lies well out into the Atlantic, extending for more than 650 miles (1,000km) from the east coast of Florida to the southeastern tip of Cuba. Include every sandbank and every reef that juts out from the sea and the Bahamas consist of about 700 islands and more than 2,500 cays ('cay' is pronounced 'key' and is derived from the Spanish word *cayo* meaning 'small island').

The total land area of the Bahamas is estimated at about 5,300 sq.miles (14,000 sq.km). The islands are of various sizes, but the landscapes are very

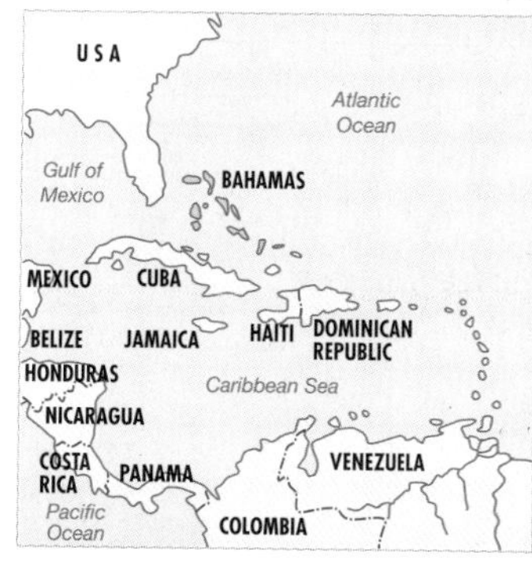

Swampy Lake Killarney

similar: low, thick pine forests, swamps overgrown with mangroves, lagoons and brackish lakes, scarcely a hill to speak of – the highest point is the 206-ft (63-m) Mount Alvernia on Cat Island – and miles and miles of fine, bright sandy beaches. There are hardly any rivers on the islands, just a few freshwater lakes. Appreciable quantities of below-ground water are rare.

The foundations for the Bahamas are the Little and Great Bahama Banks, huge chalk plateaux which are bordered by deep sea lanes. The Straits of Florida separate the islands in the northwest from the north American mainland; two other main channels, the Northwest Providence Channel and the Northeast Providence Channel, separate Andros, with an area of 2,160 sq miles (6,000 sq km) the biggest island in the group, and New Providence from Grand Bahama and the Abaco Islands; the deepest channel (5,900ft/1,800m in depth), Tongue of the Ocean, runs between Andros and the Exumas; in the far southwest, the Old Bahama Channel lies between the Bahamas and Cuba.

Great Exuma – on the Tropic of Cancer

The Tropic of Cancer runs across the Great Bahama Bank and through Great Exuma. Acklins Island and Crooked Island, Great Inagua, Mayaguana Island and Ragged Island lie below this line and are often lumped together and described as the 'Southern Islands'.

Recent research on the emergence of what is known as the Bahama Plate proves that north America drifted west away from the African continent about 165 million years ago. The Bahamas micro-plate separated at about the same time and came to rest between Florida and Cuba. In the millions of years that followed, shallow-water sediment, mainly limestone sand, accumulated on the surface, while the base continued to sink, thus forming the massive 3,250-ft (1,000-m) Bahama Banks.

Ice-Age dunes, now sandstone

Climatic changes during the next two million years, principally the four Ice Ages, created the morphological structure of the modern Bahamian archipelago. During the Ice Ages the water level around the Bahama Banks fell, exposing a large island formation, sometimes known as the *Isla Grande* or the Great Bahamian Island. If man had lived on the Bahamas during the last Ice Age, then he would have been able to walk over dry land from the Bimini Islands in the north to Long Island 370 miles (600km) away. As the glaciers melted, the sea level rose and broad coastal strips and low-lying land were flooded and lost to the sea. The higher regions were separated from each other and the islands were formed.

The *Isla Grande* was devastated as the water level rose, becoming a barren, arid landscape where only sparse, desert vegetation could survive. But when the rain penetrated into the limestone, chalk particles broke off and created caves through which the water could run underground.

Underwater adventure

The extensive underwater cave complexes and the numerous 'blue holes' occurred as a result of this limestone cratering. Blue holes, which can be found both on land and at sea, are simply the cave entrances. Those that are found at sea are called 'ocean holes'. 'Boiling holes' are also found on the Bahamas, so called because they give the impression that the water in them is at a rolling boil. In fact, as the swells and tides change the water level, the resulting pressure forces water and air in through the cave entrances, and a mixture of the two comes bubbling out through the openings.

Blue holes are not unusual on the Bahamas. On Andros alone there are reckoned to be about 400 of them and for the unwary visitor they come as something of a shock because they appear to be bottomless shafts.

Spectacular blue hole

Climate and when to go

The Bahamas are a good holiday destination at any time of the year. The sub-tropical to tropical location, the Trade Winds and the Gulf Stream help to maintain relatively even temperatures. During the course of the year, the range is within 68–86°F (20–30°C) during the day and 62–70°F (17–21°C) at night. Seawater temperatures fluctuate between 73°F (23°C) in February and 82°F (28°C) in August. The skies above the Bahamas are usually blue and cloudless. It rarely rains during the six months of winter; it is during the months of June and August that the tropical downpours can be heavy, although usually short-lived. The southern islands receive about half as much rain as New Providence and the northern islands.

Between June and November the Bahamas, like the other Caribbean islands and the southern states of the US, are on hurricane alert. The storms are most likely to occur between August and October. In 1992 the islands of Eleuthera, Harbour Island, Spanish Wells, Bimini and the Berry Islands, along with southern Florida, were devastated by Hurricane Andrew. Statistics collected over the past 90 years indicate that the Bahamas can expect a hurricane of such ferocity every nine years. An accurate early-warning system now gives plenty of time for visitors to leave the islands before the storms arrive.

Doing the daily chores

Summer is the best time for tourists with a limited budget: accommodation, leisure and sporting facilities can be between 20 and 60 percent cheaper than in winter. This is because many tourists stay away in summer because they fear, mistakenly, that it will be too hot, and because of the possibility of hurricanes, although the early warning system makes this far less of a threat than it once was.

Population

Only 30 islands are inhabited. The vast majority of the 255,000 inhabitants live in the two main cities – Nassau on New Providence Island (pop. 172,000) and Freeport on Grand Bahama Island (pop. 41,000). About 80 percent of Bahamians are black, about 3 percent Asian or Hispanic, and around 17 percent are white. Many of the so-called African Bahamians are descendants of African slaves brought to the islands by early settlers and slave owners who needed their physical labor to develop the land into vast profit-making plantations. They are now spread across all strata of society.

The white Bahamians are descendants of immigrants from Europe and the US. In the middle of the 17th century the 'Eleutheran Adventurers', a few British Puritans who had previously lived on Bermuda, arrived here seeking greater religious freedom and settled on an island which they christened Eleuthera, the Greek word for freedom. In the second half of the 18th century another group in search of a new home established themselves on the Bahamas: they were Loyalists who no longer wished to live in North America when it ceased to be a British colony. The American Civil War (1861–65) brought a new wave of immigrants from the southern states. And there are still a few whites who will proudly claim to trace their roots back to some pirate, buccaneer or smuggler.

...and ye shall find

Religion

The official religion of the Bahamas is Anglican, but there are many Catholics, Methodists, Baptists and members of the Greek Orthodox Church. A number of other religions, from Muslim to Jewish, are also well represented.

Language

Bahamians speak English, and although the dialect can sometimes mean differences in emphasis and pronunciation, most people soon get used to it.

Society

Income and education determine social ranking, but roots and skin color also play a part. True, the white minority ruled for many years and are not inclined to forget it, but a peaceful social revolution here has helped the black majority achieve real political power and move towards equal status with the former governors of the region.

There are many very rich and powerful people living on the Bahamas. The majority of them have earned their privileged position through hard work and a little bit of luck, but in some cases it has been won through smuggling (sometimes drugs). The next social group is the broad middle tier of society who enjoy a comfortable lifestyle, then comes a relatively poor and less well educated class, who often struggle to makes ends meet. At the very bottom of the social ladder are immigrants from the poorest Caribbean islands, Haiti and the Dominican Republic. These 'guest workers' have often gained illegal entry into the country. While they are widely regarded as hard-working people, they are usually poorly educated, speak very little English and live isolated existences on the outskirts of towns.

Wealthy port of call

Uptown girls

Economy

Compared to all the neighboring states, the standard of living on the Bahamas is very high, with annual per capita income estimated at around $11,000. The most important source of income is undoubtedly tourism. Around 3.7 million people visit the island and in most years tourism nets over half of Gross Domestic Product (GDP). About half of the Bahamas working population – around 50,000 – are employed in the tourist trade.

Banking and finance is also an important sector. About 10 percent of GDP derives from this branch of the econ-

Tourism is the most important source of income

omy and it employs about 3,500 people. Since the end of the 1960s, the Bahamas have been an ideal center for finance-related companies, because secrecy is guaranteed and deposits and investment income are tax-free.

Keeping a watchful eye

In recent years, the government has tried to establish a light industry base through the production of beer, rum and pharmaceuticals. Fishing and agriculture are relatively low priorities as the yields are only sufficient to meet the needs of the islanders.

Historically, smuggling, racketeering, piracy and wrecking (plundering wrecked ships) played an important role in the economy of the Bahamas. During the American Civil War the islanders did good business with the blockade runners, and smuggling alcohol to the United States brought huge profits during the prohibition years between the two world wars.

In present-day Bahamas, it is drugs such as crack, cocaine and marijuana which are carried by boat or flown into the US. This type of smuggling is neither so public nor so socially acceptable as in the 'good old days', but drug smuggling as a way of life thrives, despite the joint efforts of the US and Bahamian authorities.

Politics

After around 250 years of British colonial rule, on July 10, 1973 the Commonwealth of the Bahama Islands received its independence and a new nation was born. It adopted a ministerial form of democratic government in which the black majority is represented in proportion to its numerical strength within the population.

At one time national affairs were run by the Bay Street Boys, the prosperous white minority that also controlled the economy of the Bahamas. But in the second half of the 20th century, the black majority developed a new politi-

The Parliament building in Nassau

cal consciousness. They organized themselves into political parties, such as the Progressive Liberal Party (PLP) and a bitter political struggle began, with white conservatives, members of the United Bahamian Party (UBP), desperate to hold on to power. In 1963, after a series of politically motivated strikes and general unrest, the British government intervened and a new, democratic constitution was formulated.

The UBP retained its hold on power in elections the following year, but before long a controversial young politician by the name of Lynden Pindling started to make waves. After a period in which the PLP boycotted parliamentary sittings, new elections were unexpectedly called in 1967. Shortly afterwards, a coalition government led by the ebullient Pindling took over the reins of power in Nassau. Many still give him, his followers and even the defeated Bay Street Boys credit for engineering this political change without violence and by democratic means.

A few years later another important change took place in a peaceful, democratic manner. Despite the fears of members of the Free National Movement (FNM), the descendant of the UBP, who thought that ending British colonial rule would herald economic decline, the Bahamas gained its independence on July 10, 1973.

A new political era began, under the leadership of Lynden Pindling, and lasted for nearly 20 years. In the elections of 1992, Pindling was forced out, exhausted and weakened by corruption within his party. Hubert Ingraham, leader of the FNM, became the new prime minister.

The coat of arms

The Bahamas since the 1992 election

In his election campaign, Ingraham promised not only to carry out reforms if he won power but also to tackle the increasing corruption among government officials. The signs are that his policies brought more than just a breath of fresh air to Nassau. The 60-year monopoly of the Broadcasting Corporation of the Bahamas (ZNS) has been broken. Various adjustments have been made to taxation, commercial and property law to ensure that the Bahamas – already well known as a tax haven – becomes even more attractive to foreign investors.

The Ministry of Tourism has privatized many of the state-run hotels and holiday complexes and is also trying to boost tourism on the Out Islands. Work is now going ahead on improving the islands' infrastructure and the badly potholed roads are being resurfaced. In education, more teachers have been appointed, new buildings provided and compulsory schooling extended from 8 to 10 years. Last but not least, Ingraham has introduced tougher measures to deal with drug smuggling and is co-operating more closely with the US coastguards.

Boarding party

Historical Highlights

Peace-loving Indians, Spaniards in search of conquest, unscrupulous pirates, pioneers intent on religious freedom, loyal monarchists, crafty smugglers and adventurers, the descendants of African slaves and businessmen looking for wealth and power – all these groups have made their contribution to the turbulent history of the Bahamas.

8th–14th centuries Members of the peaceful Lucayan tribe (*see page 13*), whose language was related to that of the Arawak Indians, are gradually forced to flee to the Bahamas to escape from the warrior Caribs found in the southern Caribbean.

1492 Christopher Columbus, commissioned by the Spanish royal family to seek a sea route to India, becomes the first European to set foot on a New World island, which he names San Salvador. Within 25 years the native Lucayans are completely wiped out.

1513 Ponce de Leon discovers the Gulf Stream.

1629 England claims the Bahamas.

1648 A group of British settlers arrives from Bermuda. These 'Eleutheran Adventurers' are the first Europeans to make their home in the Bahamas on an island they christen Eleuthera (Greek = freedom).

1656 A settlement is founded on New Providence on the site of modern Nassau.

1718 Captain Woodes Rogers is appointed Governor General of the Bahamas by the British crown. Rogers expels the pirates from Nassau and tries to establish order on the other islands.

1729 The first representative assembly of Bahamians convenes, instigated by Rogers on New Providence.

1780 Frank Spense, a slave, arrives with a group of loyalists. He creates a ministry which becomes the Bahamian Anglican Church.

1783 Influx of Loyalists, after America ceases to be a British colony.

1834 The 'United Kingdom Emancipation Act' frees all slaves within the British Empire. It takes a few years before the letter of the law is met on the Bahamas.

1861–5 The American Civil War brings a degree of prosperity to the islands as Nassau becomes an important harbor for blockade runners who keep the Southern states supplied with food despite the embargo imposed by the North. Economic depression returns with the end of the Civil War .

1919–33 The Prohibition era in the US leads to a flourishing trade in alcohol smuggling. Prosperity returns to the islands. The Bay Street Boys rise to prominence.

1955 Wallace Groves, founder of the Grand Bahama Port Authority, gets approval for the Hawksbill Creek Agreement, creating a tax-free haven which becomes Freeport-Lucaya.

1940 The Duke of Windsor, who had renounced his claim to the British throne, is appointed Governor of the Bahamas.

1962 Women gain the vote.

1964 The Bahamas are granted the right to self-government. Sir Roland Symonette becomes the first prime minister.

1967 Representing the black majority the Progressive Liberal Party (PLP) under Lynden Pindling wins a closely fought election.

July 10, 1973 The Union Jack is lowered in Nassau after three centuries of British colonial rule. The Bahamas become an independent state but retain close ties with Britain.

1992 After 25 years of rule by Pindling and the PLP, Hubert Ingraham and his Free National Movement (FNM) win power at the ballot box.

The early settlers

The earliest known settlers in the Bahamas were the Lucayans, a tribe that originated in South America and spoke a language similar to the Arawak Indians. Like many later arrivals from

Europe and North America, the Lucayans (from Lukku-Cairi, an Indian name meaning 'island people') found their way to the Bahamas while searching for a place of safety. Between the 8th and 14th centuries the Lucayans, a peace-loving people, were forced to escape from the aggressive and warlike Caribs based in the Greater Antilles. They finally withdrew completely from the Caribbean and established a new home on the Bahamas archipelago. Here they managed to survive, although still under threat from their neighbors to the south. Although the Lucayans were proficient with bows, arrows and spears, they preferred to use them for hunting animals rather than for killing fellow human beings.

During the few centuries that the 40,000 or so Lucayans were able to live in relative peace, they built boats and fished the coastal waters. The sea was the focal point of their lives as it was the main source of food. Their diet was supplemented by the few products they were able to cultivate in the meager soil. These early settlers also made jewelry and were skilled weavers and potters. But only a few hundred years after their flight to the Bahamas the Lucayans' peaceful lifestyle came to an abrupt and brutal end.

The enemy this time was not their neighbors but the Spanish conquistadores from the Old World many thousands of miles to the east. When the Spaniards, under the leadership of Christopher Columbus, arrived in October 1492, the future of the Lucayan culture was in jeopardy. The Spanish soon turned their backs on the Bahamas when they failed to find the gold they had hoped for, and turned their attention to the island of Hispaniola to the southeast. When they found the precious metal there, the hard and dangerous work in the gold mines was given to the Taínos, the native Indians. However, they soon fell victim to the backbreaking work and the imported European diseases against which they had no resistance. Realising that the wealth promised by the lucrative mines was increasingly threatened by labor shortages, the Spaniards decided to import Lucayan workers from the Bahamas. Some died fighting for their freedom, others perished on the journey. Any that were left met the same fate as the Taínos: they were either worked to death in the mines or else they succumbed to European diseases.

Within 25 years, the Spanish conquistadores had wiped out the Lucayan people and the beautiful Bahama islands were left uninhabited for many years to come.

Christopher Columbus and the Bahamas

Seafarer and adventurer Christopher Columbus (Cristobal Colón) spent many years trying to convince the Spanish royal family that a sea route to India existed. He had a plan and needed a patron. The prospect of a quick route to the land where delicious spices grew and vast quantities of gold and silver could be exploited finally convinced the Spanish monarch. In the middle of 1492 Columbus set sail across the Atlantic with two caravels, the *Nina* and *Pinta*, in his flagship the *Santa María*. They sailed westward for four long weeks before sighting birds, a sure sign of land.

On the 12 October 1492, the first Europeans set foot in the New World. It was probably on the small island of San Salvador (Holy Saviour), but Columbus believed that he had found the western route to India.

For the inhabitants of the island, the Lucayans, the arrival of the Europeans was to change their lives – indeed, it was the beginning of the end for them. Within 25 years, the whole tribe had been wiped out.

After landing on San Salvador, Columbus sailed south and at the end of December 1492 he reached an island which he named Hispaniola (now Haiti and the Dominican Republic). His ship, the *Santa María*, went aground on a reef, and Columbus's life was saved by the Hispaniolan native Indians. In the meantime Martín Pinzón, the captain of the *Pinta*, and his crew were embarking on a series of murderous forays. The Spanish adventurers wanted gold – as quickly as possible and in large quantities – and the inhabitants of the Caribbean islands were not treated with any great compassion. Columbus, impressed by the innocence and purity of the natives, disapproved of the way in which his men treated the indigenous population, but apparently did little to stop them.

At the beginning of 1493 Columbus returned to Spain, to be greeted with high honors and a handsome reward.

Five hundred years later, historians researching Columbus's exploits are not certain that the island of San Salvador was the site of the first landing. The logbook of the *Santa María* no longer exists so it is the chronicles left by the chaplain Bartolomé de Las Casas which are given greatest credence. The islands resemble each other very closely and current names do not correspond with those used by the native Indians or the Spanish conquerors.

New arrival in Nassau
Preceding pages:
Safe bathing and sandy beaches

Route 1

New Providence

This island, 21 miles (34km) long and 7 miles (11km) wide, is home to two-thirds of the population of the Bahamas. It is often equated with the capital Nassau, but in fact it has two faces. Beyond the hustle and bustle of the capital, with its cruise ships, tourist facilities, banks and governmental buildings, as well as the popular resorts of Cable Beach and Paradise Island (*see page 22*), life in the hinterland moves at a relaxed and leisurely pace.

Atlantis Hotel, Paradise Island

Most of the settlements are situated on the coast, as nature makes few concessions to those who choose to live in the interior. Desolate areas of mosquito-infested swamp surround Lake Killarney, and elsewhere the landscape is characterised by dense groves of dwarf palms and low-growing pines. Years of unrestrained growth around Nassau have resulted in the northeast of the island being the only area that is relatively densely populated.

For many years it was pirates and buccaneers who wielded the real power in the Bahamas and thus determined not only the fate of Nassau, but that of all the other islands (*see page 17*). From the middle of the 18th century, the Puritan settlers from New England and envoys of the British crown were officially in charge, but they were not able to eradicate fully the pernicious influence of piracy and the men who recognized no law but their own. In the 1860s, during the American Civil War, and also during the Prohibition era in the 1920s, the island became a smugglers' haven. But these swashbuckling days are long gone, and the entrepreneurs of today carve out a legal, but perhaps equally lucrative, role as international financiers and holiday hosts.

★★ Nassau

Whenever the Bahamas are mentioned, Nassau automatically springs to mind. Even the Bahamians say Nassau when what they really mean is New Providence Island. The capital of the archipelago may not truly reflect the soul of the Bahamas, but one thing is certain: the heart of the island beats strongly here. Whether it is politics, culture, tourism or finance, Nassau is the focal point. Proof of this can be seen on the streets, in the markets and in the shops, by the harbor and at the holiday centers. Despite the hustle and bustle and cosmopolitan atmosphere, Nassau has retained much of the old charm from when it was a hide-out for buccaneers and pirates.

Busy streets and beautiful old buildings

History

When the first Puritan settlers arrived in 1666, New Providence was known as Sayle's Island. The natural harbor just outside Nassau was the ideal choice for a settlement and the town they founded was christened Charles Town. In 1695, in honor of the Prince of Orange-Nassau, later to become King William III of England, the town was renamed Nassau. From the 17th to the 19th centuries, the Anglican church imported by the devout Puritan settlers dominated – not just in everyday life, but also in politics and commerce.

For many decades, however, there was another source of power and influence. Buccaneers strode the streets of the new settlement, enjoying life on land and making the most of the wealth acquired through their lawless exploits and adventures on the high seas. Bay Street, close to the harbor, became their headquarters.

The pirates' lair, which housed over 300 inhabitants in the late 17th century, was frequently attacked by Spanish, French and American warships, and a number of forts were built for protection. In the 18th century, the English became aware of what was going on in their Bahamian colony. They sent envoys to clean up the islands and rid the region of the pillaging pirates.

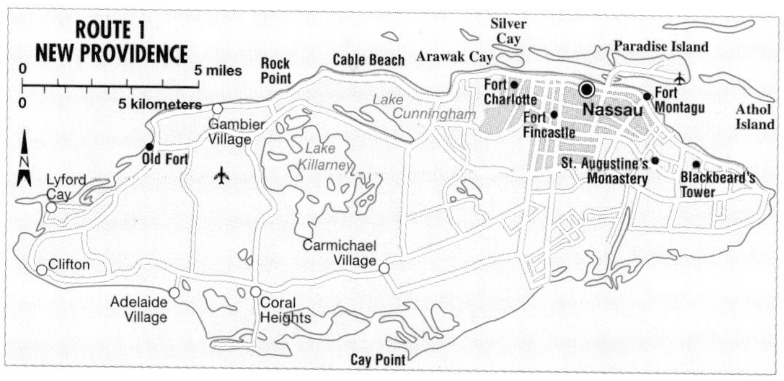

In 1718 the privateer Woodes Rogers was appointed as the islands' first royal governor. His first official duty was to enlist anyone who was willing to bring some semblance of order to the town of Nassau – even some of the buccaneers who were the cause of the trouble in the first place. Many years later, Governor William Shirley surveyed the town and drained the swamps where the dangerous mosquitoes bred. Subsequently, a number of other representatives of the British royal household sought to govern Nassau, which in the second half of the 18th century became dominated by Loyalists who fled from the American mainland when it ceased to be a British colony.

By the middle of the 19th century, anarchy once again reigned on the island. In the turmoil of the American Civil War, Nassau became a base for blockade runners who brought prosperity to the town and made Nassau a fashionable playground for the rich and beautiful. But with the end of the war in the United States the flow of money into Nassau ceased and the good life came to an end. Only the Prohibition era of the 1920s inspired prosperity again. The alcohol ban in the United States reawakened the islanders' passion for smuggling. Their dry neighbors in the west obtained the liquor they craved and Nassau enjoyed a cash bonanza from the illicit trade.

The turbulent years of pirates, colonialism and smuggling are now long gone, but in the heart of the old town the tales that are told still seem relevant today. Most inhabitants of Nassau now earn their living from less risky pursuits. It is a reputable financial and banking center and also the hub of the thriving Bahamian tourist industry. However, the cat and mouse game continues. Now it is the drug smugglers with their light aircraft and speedboats who try to outsmart the US coastguards.

Relic of pirate days

American coastguard on alert

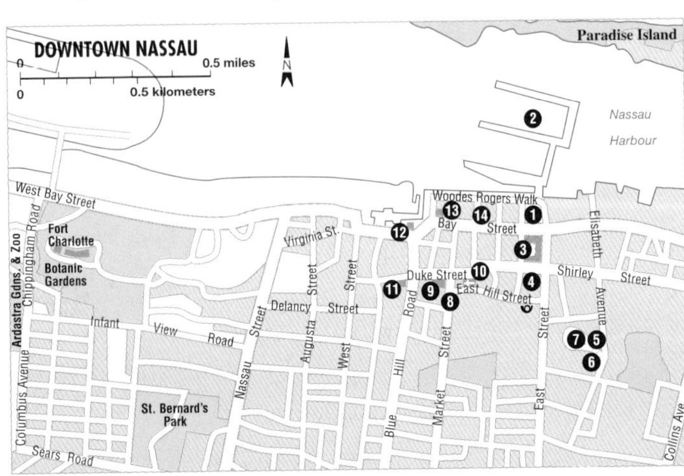

A leisurely way to see Nassau

City tour

The main historical sights of Nassau are concentrated within a relatively small area and can easily be covered on foot – but do wear a stout, comfortable pair of shoes. An early start is advisable, as the only appreciable hill in the town, which affords a good view of Fort Fincastle, really ought to be climbed before midday, after which the heat of the sun becomes extreme. A long, relaxed lunch is recommended.

Prince George Wharf

The ideal starting point for a tour of the old town is **Rawson Square** ❶, the centre of Nassau. This bustling square serves as the link between **Prince George Wharf** ❷, anchorage for the impressive cruise liners, and the rows of shops along Bay Street. To save on shoe leather and conserve energy, visitors can always tour the old town in a 'surrey', a brightly-decorated, horse-drawn carriage.

Opposite Rawson Square is another square, which is probably one of Nassau's most-photographed spots. **Parliament Square** ❸ is quite small, and contains a statue of the young Queen Victoria, flanked on three sides by government buildings dating from around 1800. The first edifice on the left is the pink-painted **House of Assembly**, which accommodates the longest-surviving parliament in the New World. Parliament Street, with its Georgian-style, pastel-shaded houses resembles a row of enlarged doll's houses more than the government quarter of an important financial metropolis.

Queen Victoria

Walk southwards and on the left you will see the **Supreme Court**, where the highest court in the Bahamas meets. Next door is the octagonal **Nassau Public Library and Museum**. It was built in 1797 as a prison. Although for the past 120 years it has been used as an archive for books, old prints, maps and photos, the small prison cells have

The Library used to be a prison

The Queen's Staircase

Fort Fincastle never saw battle

lost none of their oppressive atmosphere. The library also houses an exhibition about the Lucayans (*see page 13*).

Opposite the library, on the other side of Shirley Street, is the site of the legendary, but now demolished, **Royal Victoria Hotel** ❹. Built around 1860, it acquired a reputation as the finest hotel in the tropics and was frequented by smugglers, spies, royalty, playboys and visitors from Europe and the United States, as well as the top echelons of Bahamian society. For a century it was the top venue for Nassau's social occasions and meetings of influential businessmen. By 1971 the hotel had lost its cachet, had ceased to be profitable and was closed down.

Continue along Shirley Street in the direction of Elizabeth Avenue, where on the right the **Queen's Staircase** ❺ has been carved out of the cliff. Slaves chiseled out the steps,which were named in honor of Queen Victoria. Walkers will be glad they chose a comfortable pair of shoes if, after climbing the 65 steps, they decide to ascend the 125-ft (38-m) **Water Tower** ❻. Built in 1928, it offers a splendid view over Nassau, the busy cruise ship harbor and offshore Paradise Island. At the foot of the water tower lies ★ **Fort Fincastle** ❼ (Monday to Saturday 9am–4pm). Lord Dunmore's castle dates from 1793 and resembles the bow of a ship, but the light-gray fortifications never saw battle.

A narrow footpath descends to Sands Avenue which then leads via East Street into East Hill Street, passing

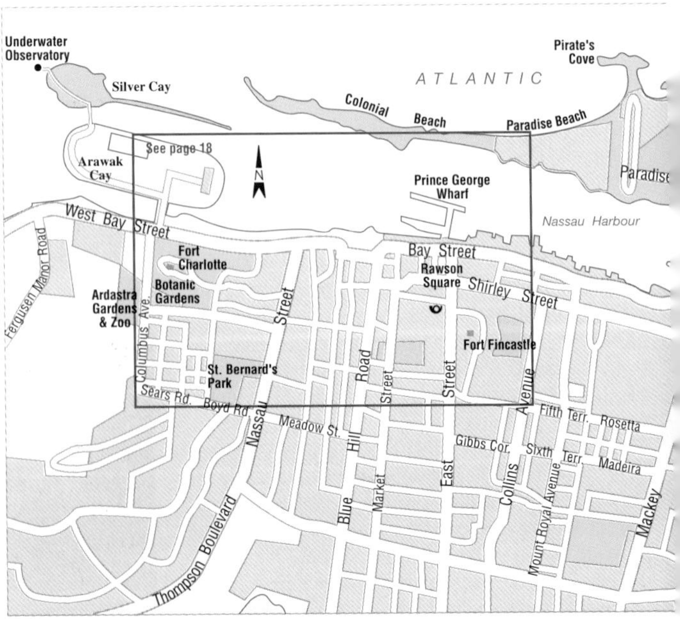

Underwater Observatory
Silver Cay
ATLANTIC
Colonial Beach
Paradise Beach
Pirate's Cove
Paradise
Arawak Cay
See page 18
N
Prince George Wharf
Nassau Harbour
West Bay Street
Fort Charlotte
Bay Street
Rawson Square
Shirley Street
Botanic Gardens
Ardastra Gardens & Zoo
Fergusen Manor Road
Columbus Ave.
Fort Fincastle
St. Bernard's Park
Sears Rd.
Boyd Rd.
Nassau Street
Meadow St.
Blue Hill Road
Market Street
East Street
Elizabeth Avenue
Fifth Terr.
Rosetta
Gibbs Cor.
Sixth Terr.
Madeira
Collins
Mount Royal Avenue
Mackey
Thompson Boulevard

the new **General Post Office**. **Gregory's Arch** ❽, a tunnel named after James Gregory, governor of the Bahamas from 1849 to 1854, can be seen at the end of East Hill Street. This passageway, which cuts through **Prospect Ridge,** links what was then the rich and poor quarters of the town. Most of Nassau's white population lived on the side facing the sea, while their black employees lived 'over the hill'. Every night the black workers had to leave the white residential area where they worked and climb over the hill to their own bleak huts. The construction of the tunnel in 1850 eased their journey home. Viewed from the top of Prospect Ridge, the difference between the two communities is still all too apparent.

Follow Market Street down the hill towards the sea. On the left stands the grand **Government House** ❾, official home of the representative of the British monarch, a post which is now strictly ceremonial. In front of the pink villa – built in 1801 in classical style – stands a statue of Christopher Columbus.

St Andrew's Kirk Presbyterian Church ❿ is situated only about three minutes' walk away on the right-hand side of the road. The Kirk, as it is known, was the first non-Anglican church to be built on the Bahamas. It was constructed in 1810 and has been altered a number of times since then.

The first signs of fatigue may well be manifesting themselves by now, so why not take a break in the small, but

Government House

Harbor view

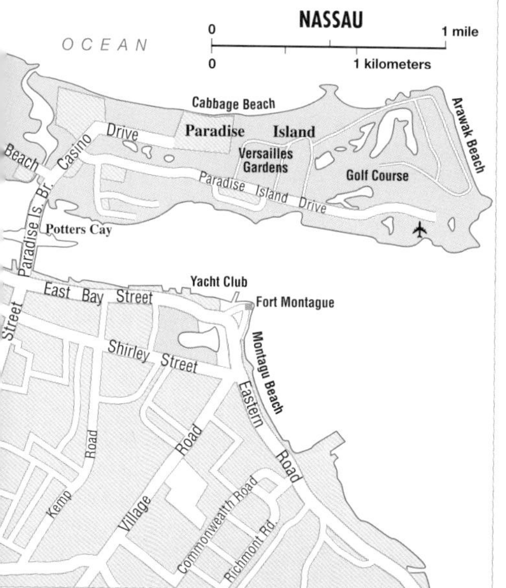

The Graycliff Hotel

excellent **Graycliff Hotel** ⓫ and restaurant on the corner of Hill Street and Blue Hill Road. The Georgian-style building dates from 1720, but it rose to prominence in the 1920s when it was run by a lady friend of gangster Al Capone. It was later taken over by Lord and Lady Dudley who attracted guests with aristocratic backgrounds such as the Duke and Duchess of Windsor.

Suitably refreshed, continue down Cumberland Street, the extension of Blue Hill Road, and past the **British Colonial Hotel** ⓬. This elegant building was constructed in 1923 by Harry Oakes, who owned a third of the island and was the most powerful man in the Bahamas at that time. It occupies the spot where Fort Nassau once stood.

Vendue House ⓭ (Monday to Friday 10am–5pm, Saturday 10am–2pm) stands opposite the hotel at the start of Bay Street. This is one of the oldest buildings in the town and was formerly used as a trading post for slaves. It has been converted into a museum and now houses an exhibition on slavery in the Bahamas.

Bountiful Bay Street

But enough of old Nassau. Long live new Nassau with its duty-free Caribbean-style shopping paradise. **Bay Street** extends for 1½ miles (2km) and is lined with shops selling jewelry, perfumes and porcelain, plus department stores stacked high with goods for the cruise passengers who sometimes overwhelm the town. The **Straw Market** ⓮ is often the busiest spot. Here Bahamian women sell hand-made products, such as hats, mats, baskets and bags.

The Straw Market is great fun

Once back at Rawson Square, take **Woodes Rogers Walk** through to **Prince George Wharf** ❷ where there are often several cruise ships moored. At night the decks are illuminated and the whole scene is a glittering sight. At the entrance to the harbor, a customs warehouse contains the **Junkanoo Expo**. This simple but gleaming exhibition provides a taster for Junkanoo, the traditional carnival-style festivities that take place throughout the Bahamas on 26 December and 1 January.

Junkanoo Expo

Excursion: Cable Beach and Paradise Island

Visitors who arrive with a hotel already booked in New Providence – or Nassau as it is known in local parlance – will almost certainly find themselves staying in one of the two main tourist centers, either Cable Beach or Paradise Island. Both resorts offer everything the international traveler could possibly wish for: crystal-clear water, fine beaches, a full range of sporting activities on land and on sea, shopping galore, hotels and restaurants in every price category, gambling casinos, cabarets and shows, and countless bars and nightclubs. What is sadly lacking is any real sense of the Caribbean. If it were not for the Bahamian dishes on the menus and the hotel-organized Junkanoo evenings (*see page 90*), visitors could easily mistake these two tourist meccas for any other major resort in the world.

It is understandable, therefore, that **Cable Beach** is sometimes known as the Riviera of the Bahamas. This coastal strip west of Nassau was developed in the 1950s purely with tourism in mind. The name is derived from the point where the first cable connection from the US mainland arrived in 1892. Rows of hotels now overlook the immaculate beach. The huge **Carnival's Crystal Palace Resort and Casino**, the largest casino in the Caribbean, is also one of the best-known hotels.

Paradise Island is only 4 miles (6km) long and is linked to Nassau by a toll bridge. Up until 1959 it was still known by the rather less romantic name of Hog Island, but the exposed position of the island just off Nassau and its pretty beaches soon attracted attention. Initially this came from millionaires seeking peace and an exclusive address, but later also from a few astute businessmen. The latter soon turned the island into a lively, international tourist complex. Paradise Island is now one of the best-known tourist centers in the Caribbean. The finest beaches are all situated on the north side of the island facing the Atlantic. From a holiday point of view, the island is fully self-sufficient. Tourists who care little for local history or the everyday life of the Bahamian people need never leave the island. There are hotels, restaurants, bars, gambling casinos, sporting facilities, botanical gardens, boat trips, even a small airport. Here, tourism is geared almost exclusively to package holidaymakers and sun-worshippers. Even so, many people find it a relaxing and refreshing place to unwind and an entertaining spot to spend a vacation.

Parasailing on Cable Beach

Colorful Crystal Palace

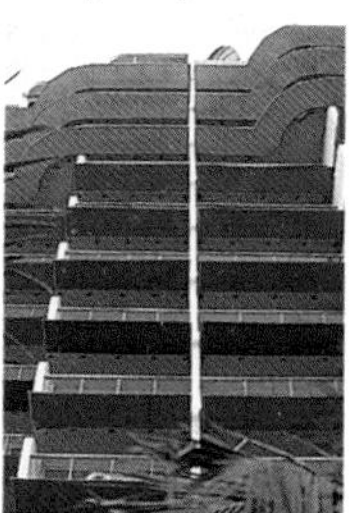

Cable Beach

Tour of the island

Unlike most of the other islands, New Providence can easily be toured by car and when doing so it is better to follow an anti-clockwise route. Start the tour in Nassau *(see page 17)*. Paradise Island and Cable Beach have devoted their full attention to tourism and can easily be avoided if you wish. But do visit if you want to experience a typical example of a lively, glitzy, well-organized tourist resorts (*see page* 22).

Within the western boundary of Nassau the impressive ★ **Fort Charlotte** comes into view. Once the biggest military base on the island, it was the pet project of the Earl of Dunmore, a former governor of the Bahamas. The structure was completed in 1789, the year of the French Revolution, and cost far more than originally planned. Yet, ironically, like its sister castle, Fort Fincastle, it never saw a shot fired in anger. In recent years it has received a facelift believed to have cost a million dollars, and its appearance is as daunting as ever.

The principal attraction at Ardastra Zoo

Visitors who prefer fauna and flora to military history should make the five-minute drive from the fort to **Ardastra Gardens and Zoo** (daily 9am–5pm), where the principal attraction is a small flock of proudly parading flamingos (performances Monday to Saturday at 11am, 2pm and 4pm).

The nearby **Botanic Gardens** (Monday to Saturday 9am–5pm) cover an area three times the size of the Ardastra Gardens, but exhibits are restricted to tropical plants.

An alternative attraction, mainly for families with children, lies on the opposite side of West Bay Street. ★ **Coral Island** (formerly Coral World, daily 9am–6pm) on Silver Cay is a small theme park which focuses on the world below the water's surface. The island is linked to New Providence by a narrow bridge. Thousands of visitors are attracted to this underwater observatory where, dry and safe behind bullet-proof glass, they can observe tropical fish, shellfish and brightly-colored flora while sharks, sea turtles and rays peer in. The more energetic can make close contact with the sea life via a snorkel trail.

Coral Island Observatory

Jet skiers at Cable Beach

On the way back to West Bay Street, take the opportunity to sample some local dishes and chat with the local traders on **Arawak Cay**, an artificial island created by the government about 25 years ago. Some local people say that it is here, by the fishermen's wooden stalls, that the best conch salad is served – it certainly is the freshest. The atmosphere on Arawak Cay hots up on Wednesday and Saturday evening when disc jockeys bring the sound of the Caribbean to life.

Head west along West Bay Street and past the hotels of **Cable Beach**. Some 6 miles (10km) beyond Arawak

Cay on the right-hand side, cinema fans may well recognize the house at Rock Point. It was used in the filming of the 1965 James Bond film *Thunderball*. In classic Bond fashion, Sean Connery recovered two stolen atom bombs from a bunch of crooks on the Bahamas – and still had time for a dry martini. On the left side of the road a few minutes further on stands the rugged entrance to **The Caves**. As the passages are dark, low and winding, it is probably better to view these unattended limestone caverns from the outside.

In contrast to the bustling island capital of Nassau, **Gambier Village** (10 miles/16km) is a simple, typically Bahamian community. Children, chicken and dogs chase around on the streets unsupervised and many of the inhabitants still live in rickety wooden huts, some painted in bright colors, others neglected and decaying. Further along the road, just minutes away, the atmosphere changes. The village of **Love** is a far more desirable district with homes for the well-off middle classes.

Lyford Cay, retreat for the super-rich

The coast road now swings round in an arc on its way to exclusive **Lyford Cay** (16 miles/26km). It is a retreat for wealthy islanders and outsiders and, of course, there is the inevitable golf course and marina. Ordinary mortals are only able to view this multi-million dollar estate from the air or from out at sea. A guard and a barrier keep uninvited visitors at bay.

Leave them to their luxury and take a trip in a submarine for a close look at life underwater. Several times a day – according to demand – the *Atlantis 1* will take up to 28 passengers underwater for just under an hour. Start out from one of the hotels in the tourist centers or from Jaws Dock on the southern edge of Lyford Cay. The submarine is anchored offshore and is just a 10-minute boat trip away.

The Atlantis surfaces

Clifton Pier (17 miles/28km) is the next stop on the island tour. The Bahamas may be famous for rum and coconut milk, but neither islanders nor tourists could survive without Kalik beer which is brewed here in the Commonwealth Brewery.

Adelaide Village (21 miles/33km) lies on the right-hand side of South West Road. This tiny, impoverished settlement was founded in 1831 by the then governor James Carmichael Smith as a home for Africans liberated from the slave ship *Rosa*. In its heyday Adelaide Village possessed its own law court, a primary school and even a prison, but the local youth have left for Nassau and the village is now a lifeless shell.

As it runs eastward Adelaide Road becomes Carmichael Road which then passes through the little town of **Carmichael Village** (26 miles/42km). From this point on, visitors are advised to stay on the main roads – particularly after dark – to avoid straying into one of the more risky areas on the southern edge of Nassau.

To reach **St Augustine's Monastery** (33 miles/52km), drivers will need to follow directions carefully. Continue along Carmichael Road and then take Blue Hill Road northwards. At the roundabout turn right into Independance Drive and after about 1 mile (1.5km) right into Prince Charles Avenue. Less than 100yds (800m) further on bear left into Soldier Road. After a few bends Soldier Road is joined by a little side road on the right. This is Bernard Road and leads to the monastery. The fortress-like building sits on top of a rise near Fox Hill, named after Samuel Fox, a slave who later became a wealthy landowner. The St Augustine Roman Catholic Monastery and College was designed as a Benedictine monastery in 1946 by John Hawes, an architect and Anglican missionary. Hawes later became a Roman Catholic and earned respect and fame on the Bahamas as Father Jerome. He lived out his life as a hermit on Cat Island.

Hibiscus flower everywhere

Not far from the monastery, down from Fox Hill, a little to the east on Yamacraw Hill Road, stands **Blackbeard's Tower**. Legend surrounds this stone edifice and many Bahamians will tell tourists that an English pirate by the name of Edward Teach, alias Blackbeard, used it as a look-out post when scouring the seas for ships to plunder.

A short distance towards the town on Village Road stands the peaceful ★ **Retreat Garden** (Tuesday and Thursday, guided tours 9am–5pm). More than 200 varieties of palms are tended in the 6-acre (4.5-ha) gardens.

A group of groupers

The last stage but one of the tour leads along East Bay Street towards the town center past **Fort Montagu**. This imposing structure, the oldest of the island's three forts, dates from 1744. Occupying a dominant position on the coast, unlike Fort Fincastle and Fort Charlotte, it saw military action and experienced defeat during the American War of Independence in 1776.

If the hustle and bustle of town life is not too much after this island tour, then ★ **Potter's Cay** is worth a visit. The busy market below Paradise Bridge, which crosses to Paradise Island, is the place to go for fresh seafood, fruit and vegetables. Fishermen from New Providence and the Out Islands sell their catch here. The varieties of fish and seafood available here include conch, a firm Bahamian favorite, which is also considered to be an aphrodisiac. The large wooden mailboats which tie up at the dock next to the market carry heavy loads of freight and passengers coming and going from the nearby harbor, adding to the hectic atmosphere that surrounds the market area.

The mailboat at Potter's Key

Route 2

Grand Bahama, warmed by the Gulf Stream

★★★ Grand Bahama

History
The Spanish christened this island *Gran Bajamar,* meaning the Great Shallows, out of respect for the dangers that the shallow water posed to their ships. During the colonial years, the hazards of the Little Bahama Bank were to prove profitable to the inhabitants of the island, as the boats that ran aground could easily be plundered for the treasures they carried. Today's inhabitants earn their living in a far more responsible way from the island's holiday guests, who are attracted by the clear waters warmed by the Gulf Stream.

Fish sheltering in brain coral

Whether it is the spotless beaches of the south coast or the bustling casinos of the island's two main resorts of Freeport and Lucaya, Grand Bahama has an almost magical appeal. Visitors should, however, not expect the same rich historical past as is found in Nassau. Across the whole island and in Freeport and Lucaya, two towns which merge almost seamlessly, it is the spirit of the new which prevails.

Visitors to the western side of Grand Bahama will soon see for themselves an important element in the island's history, for this is the only island on the Bahamas which can claim to have any industry. Many a politician would have loved to create an economic metropolis here. Proximity to Florida, only 65 miles (105km) away, promised commercial advantages, but the empty factories testify to failed investment and disappointed ambitions.

Freeport is not a town that evolved over time, but is the product of businessman Wallace Groves, who built a free port here in the 1950s. In 1955 the investment-minded

Americans signed the Hawksbill Creek Agreement with the government. Groves received 50,000 acres (20,000ha) of land, tax-free, and permission to import duty-free goods. In return, he promised to build a deep-sea harbor and to transform the island into an industrial center which would offer much-needed employment.

Freeport did enjoy a short, economic boom and Groves' company earned a fortune. But with a new Bahamas government in 1967, after the Progressive Liberal Party won the elections, and recession in the United States, the situation soon changed. By the 1970s business confidence collapsed and foreign firms left the island. But Wallace Groves, a man with tremendous foresight and energy, had already hit upon another, far more lucrative source of income – tourism. By the end of 1963 he had opened the Lucayan Beach Hotel, a luxury hotel with a gambling casino. Thus Lucaya, the prettier twin sister of the industrial port of Freeport, was born. The tourist industry is now by far the most important sector in the economy and Lucaya has become an idyllic holiday paradise. Even Freeport has had to turn to tourism, although the prime minister, Hubert Ingraham, seems to be reconsidering its role as an industrial location.

Princess Casino, Freeport

Freeport/Lucaya

The face of Freeport was scarred at birth. It is true there are some fine villas and large gardens but, outside the central area, a clear view of the beautiful landscape is blocked by factory buildings and run-down houses. The busy East Sunrise Highway links Freeport with neighboring Lucaya

Sampling the nectar

Shells for sale

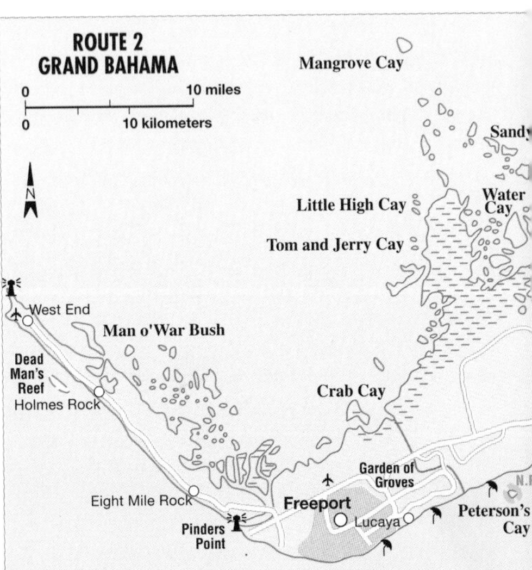

where hotel blocks dominate the skyline. The two towns run into one another and no one seems to know where one stops and the other starts. Neither of the two centers has much to offer in the way of walks and even the locals do not seem to go anywhere on foot. To cover the main sights, it is better either to hire a car or bike, or to take a bus or taxi.

International ambience at the Bazaar

The **International Bazaar** at the heart of Freeport is the principal destination for the cruise passengers who stream from their huge ships. There is little on sale here that can be described as typically Bahamian. The entrance is, in fact, shaped like an oriental arch, modelled on the Japanse traditional gate of welcome, so visitors may be a bit disorientated.The bazaar is, nonetheless, worth a visit. Over 90 shops, restaurants, stalls selling culinary delights and traditional wares from about 25 different countries make up this shoppers' paradise that dates from 1967. You can even tour the **Perfume Factory** and create your own, indivdual scent from the fragrances on offer. Across the road, for any British tourists feeling homesick, is the Winston Churchill Pub, which sells English beer and traditional pub food.

Perfume factory

The ★ **Rand Memorial Nature Centre** (Monday to Friday guided tours 10am, 2pm, 3pm, Sunday 2pm, 3pm) poses less of a threat to the pocket than the International Bazaar. This 100-acre (40-ha) wooded area between Freeport and Lucaya, run by the Bahamas National Trust, bears the name of James Rand, a former president of the

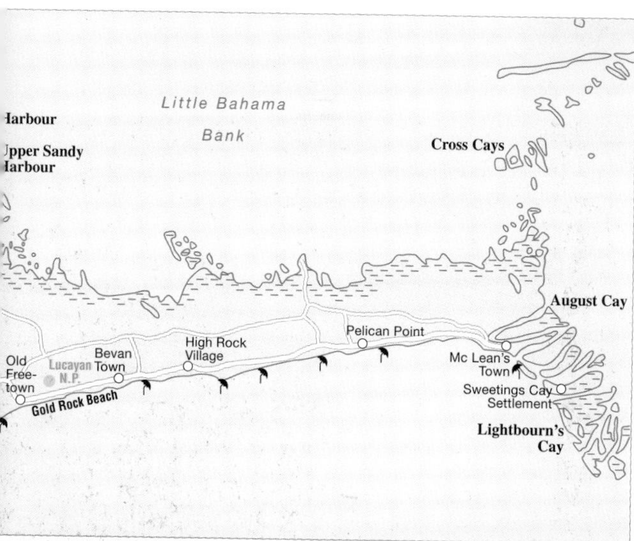

American company Remington Rand, who donated a hospital and a library to the island. Lovers of orchids will enjoy the opportunity to join one of the guided tours through this nature reserve where over 20 species of the rare flower are carefully preserved.

Explorers' paradise

The resorts of Lucaya and Freeport are actually popular with tourists for a different kind of green, one which is cut short and kept free of any wild plants. There are no fewer than five golf courses *(see page 79)* within the urban area.

The ★★ **Underwater Explorers Society** (UNEXSO) (daily 8am–6pm) in Port Lucaya *(see page 75)* has a reputation which extends way beyond the coastal waters of Grand Bahama. It is, in fact, one of the most highly respected diving centers in the world. The diving school invites 2,500 holidaymakers each year to don a mask and oxygen canister.

Facilities at the center include a diving pool some 20ft (6m) in depth with an observation window and a decompression chamber. Qualified (and very experienced) diving instructors provide courses to beginners and advanced practitioners. They claim that absolute beginners can be taught to dive in three hours. Nearby Treasure Cay is often used for diving practice.

UNEXSO is well known for the ★★ **Dolphin Experience**. Animal rights protestors campaigned against the relatively small pools in which the dolphins used to be kept, so now they enjoy the extensive facilities of Sanctuary Bay. Tourists can make the 2-mile (3-km) ferry journey across to Sanctuary Bay to see the dolphin show or to swim with the dolphins. The Dolphin Experience is often fully booked up weeks in advance during the busy holiday season. Reservations are recommended.

Dolphin Experience

Close encounter

Island tours

While Freeport and Lucaya are important in a tourist context, Grand Bahama has other things to offer. The island is flat, so the best way to explore the area around the main conurbation is by bike (*enquire at the tourist office for bike hire outlets – see page 83 of the Practical Information section for details*). **Taino Beach** (between Freeport and Lucaya), **Fortuna Beach** (Lucaya) and the **Garden of the Groves**, a botanical garden just before the Grand Lucayan Waterway are all within easy reach on two wheels. Luckily for the local wildlife, the north coast is mainly accessible only by boat. Two day trips are sufficient to cover the south coast of the island.

Bahamian blooms

Start with the shorter 31-mile (50-km) trip to the west end of the island. Follow the West Sunrise Highway out of Freeport, past the industrial and commercial district to **Hawksbill Creek** (5 miles/8km), a channel of sea which cuts across the island from the north. During the morning, fishermen stand on the bridge and sell their catch, leaving behind mounds of discarded conch shells.

A fine specimen

Small villages, which have seen better times, now line the road. Look out for signs to small shops, cafés and also blue holes (*see page 7*). Enjoy the quiet countryside as you pass and observe the everyday life of the islanders. Sometimes on a sunny Sunday morning a choir of gospel singers will emerge from one of the many village churches followed by a train of children, scrubbed clean for the morning service, who will then stand and curiously ogle any outsiders.

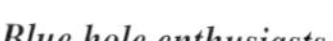

Blue hole enthusiasts

Beyond the promisingly named **Eight Mile Rock** (9 miles/14km) lies nothing more than a settlement that extends for just that – eight miles. On the coastal side of the village lies a 'boiling hole' (it is worth asking directions from one of the locals). The name derives from the water that bubbles to the surface after flowing under pressure through a system of underground caves *(see page 7)*. Another of these boiling holes, known locally as 'the chimney', lies just past Freeport Harbour at **Pinders Point**.

West End (31 miles/50km) is the oldest settlement on Grand Bahama – Lucayans, the islands' earliest inhabitants, are said to have eked out a peaceful existence here. The town enjoyed considerable prosperity during the Prohibition era because its close proximity to Florida made it an important center for alcohol smuggling. More recently the luxurious **Jack Tar Village**, with a golf course, tropical gardens and marina also brought vitality and money to this end of the island, but it closed following a damaging strike by staff. Government plans to revive not only the holiday center but the whole region include an idea to host

West End vernacular

Tropical color

a weekly street fair. **West End Move** is a lively event that should not be missed. Dancing, feasting and drinking takes place every Saturday along the promenade.

Heading east out of Freeport, visitors will find inspiring nature reserves and miles and miles of sandy beach. Given the poor roads and the many attractive spots which may tempt you, allow at least a day for this 58-mile (93-km) excursion to McLean's Town. Begin on East Sunrise Highway and make the ★ **Garden of the Groves** (6 miles/10km, Tuesday to Sunday 9am–5pm) the first stop. This romantically laid out park (12 acres/5ha) is a blaze of exotic, tropical color, and well worth a visit. Standing on a hill among waterfalls, ponds and numerous species of rare trees stands a small chapel which is often hired for wedding ceremonies. Alongside the gardens, the ★ **Grand Bahama Museum** (Tuesday to Sunday 9am–5pm) documents the history of the island and displays an interesting collection of artifacts which belonged to the Lucayan Indians and others from the buccaneering days, as well as a section on the Junkanoo, the national festival.

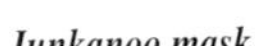

Junkanoo mask

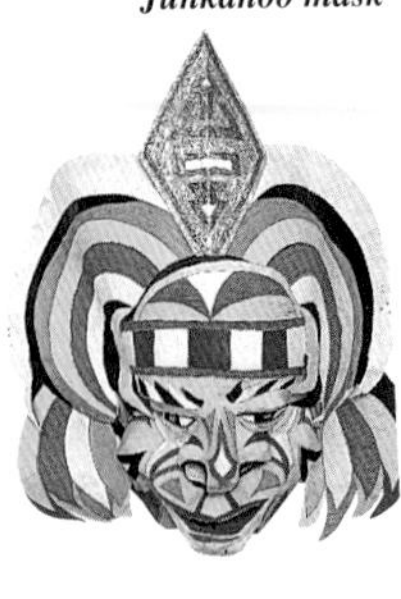

In the ★★ **Lucayan National Park**, 15 miles (24km) further east along Midshipman Road and just behind Gold Rock, lie more natural curiosities. A narrow path leads through a sparse pine forest to two 'blue holes', the only visible parts of an extensive water-filled cave system, the Lucayan Caverns. A 1-mile (1.5-km) path of wooden planks starts from the car park and winds through a thicket of mangrove and undergrowth to a delightful bathing beach named **Gold Rock Beach**.

The roadside villages on the eastbound road are of little interest: a bar, a church, a tiny shop, a fuel station and a few simple houses. **Pelican Point** (48 miles/77km) is much more attractive. Many say it is the most beautiful beach on the island. Large, not particularly easy to get to, it is pleasingly lonely, with no snack bars or watersports activities, only magnificent palm trees. A lovely spot to relax and unwind.

Excursion to Peterson's Cay

Just off the coast near Lucaya lies ★★ **Peterson's Cay National Park**. It is a tiny island which can be reached by boat from Port Lucaya. An underwater path leads snorkelers and divers through the island's spectacular reef. It is best to regard this as a separate excursion in itself, rather than part of your island tour, because it takes a whole day to really appreciate it. Take a picnic, plenty to drink and a tube of suncream.

Doctor fish

Route 3

★★ Eleuthera with Harbour Island and Spanish Wells

Connoisseurs of the Bahamas are convinced that Eleuthera is one of the most beautiful islands in the archipelago. Long and slender in shape, it lies between the shallow waters of Exuma Sound and the gloomy depths of the Atlantic Ocean. Who could resist a visit to this island with its green hills, lonely beaches and pretty fishing villages? Eleuthera also has plenty of facilities for tourists.

Irresistible Eleuthera

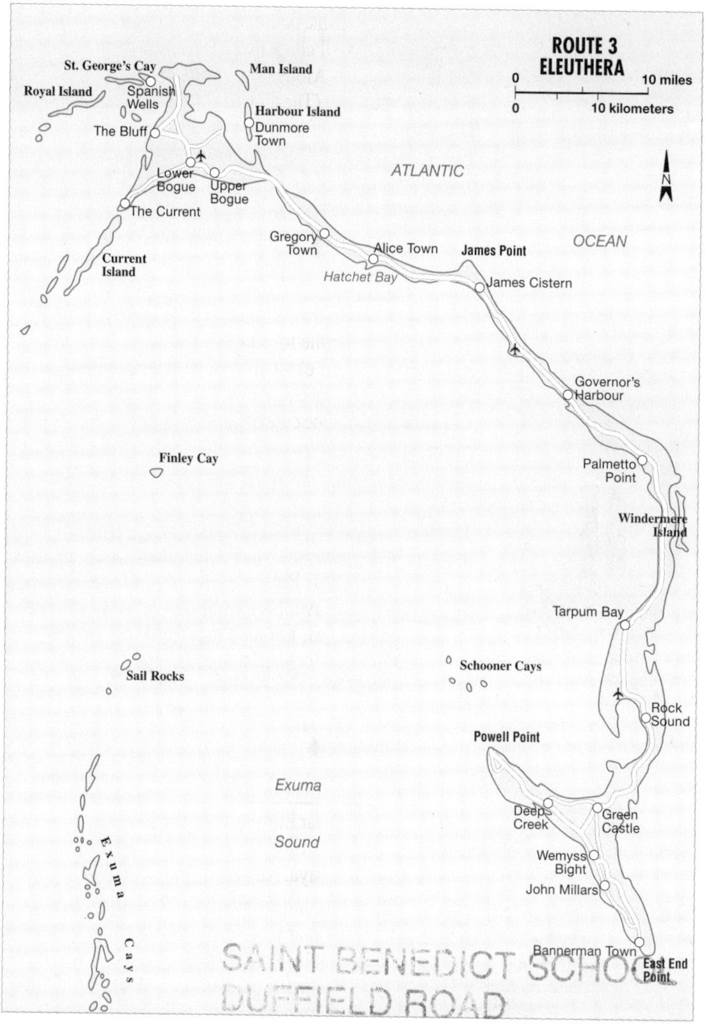

ROUTE 3
ELEUTHERA
0 10 miles
0 10 kilometers
N
St. George's Cay
Man Island
Royal Island
Spanish Wells
Harbour Island
Dunmore Town
The Bluff
Lower Bogue
Upper Bogue
ATLANTIC
OCEAN
The Current
Current Island
Gregory Town
Alice Town
James Point
Hatchet Bay
James Cistern
Governor's Harbour
Finley Cay
Palmetto Point
Windermere Island
Tarpum Bay
Schooner Cays
Sail Rocks
Rock Sound
Powell Point
Exuma
Sound
Deep Creek
Green Castle
Wemyss Bight
John Millars
Exuma Cays
Bannerman Town
East End Point

Crawfish boat at Spanish Wells

Wesley Church, Harbour Island

History

Eleuthera was the first island in the Bahamas to be resettled after the extinction of the original settlers. In 1648 a group of English Puritans set out from Bermuda in search of a place where they could follow their religious faith without fear of persecution. When their ship ran aground just off the island, they decided to stay put. They named the island Eleuthera, which is the Greek word for freedom. The island's 10,000 or so inhabitants are mainly descendants either of the original Eleutheran Adventurers, or of the Loyalists and their slaves who came to the island from the American mainland in the 18th and 19th centuries. Sometimes known as Pineapple Island, its main sources of income are agriculture, tourism and fishing.

The fact that the 105-mile (170-km) long island has three airports gives some clue to the fact that planes are now challenging boats as the main form of transport. Arriving near Rock Sound in the south of the island makes it is possible to head north to The Bluff and then return to the south, all within a day. But you may need to allow more time if you wish to include a visit to the sights on Spanish Wells in North Eleuthera and Dunmore Town on Harbour Island. The extreme south of the island, shaped like a tail-fin, has no holiday centers or hotels, and no places of particular interest.

Rock Sound is a neat little town just a mile or two south of the airport. It used to be known as Wreck Sound, as many of its earlier inhabitants earned their living from plundering the ships which frequently ran aground on the reefs and sandbanks off Eleuthera.

It is fun to browse in Rock Sound's little shops which sell handicrafts and *objets d'art* made by the local residents. In the middle of the town is the famous ★ **Ocean Hole**, a huge round 'blue hole' 250ft (75m) across. At first sight it just looks like a lake but, in fact, it is linked by underwater tunnels to the Atlantic. Grouper and snapper fish inhabit the pool, living on the food thrown to them by tourists.

Local artisan

Follow the Queen's Highway north to **Tarpum Bay**. A number of locally respected artists, such as MacMillan Hughes and Mal Flanders, live in the sleepy little fishing villages – in fact, Hughes owns a castle, which sits on top of a hill. Their watercolors and oil paintings reflect life on the island. Continue along the road, past dense pine forests and you will see **Windermere Island**, an exclusive, private island that is visible from the main road. Wealthy incomers have built their luxury villas here.

Governor's Harbour, further on, was where the original Eleutheran Adventurers settled when they arrived in the 17th century, after first camping out in the caves at **Preacher's Cove** in the extreme north of the island. The old, wooden, Victorian-style houses that cling to the hill above the port make an interesting focal point for a short stroll through the town. In the 19th century, when pineapples and citrus fruit were exported to north America, the little town was one of the busiest and most prosperous settlements on the Bahamas. Today the arrival of the mailboat is the main weekly event. Worth seeking out are the 19th-century **St Patrick's Anglican Church** and the stately **Commissioner's House** in the heart of the town.

The arrival of the mailboat is the main event

An extremely unusual sight in the Bahamas lies about 30 miles (50km) further north. Huge silos, leftovers from the once flourishing **Hatchet Bay Farm,** which was famous for its Angus cattle herd, line both sides of the road. The harbor at **Hatchet Bay** is reckoned to be one of the best in the Bahamas; yachts and charter boats moor here. Naturalists, or anyone unperturbed by dingy caves and bats, will usually find someone in the village willing, for a small fee, to light a way through **Hatchet Bay Cave,** where leaf-nosed bats breed.

About 3 miles (5km) from the caves is a beach which many rate as being among the 10 best surfing beaches in the world. Known simply as **Surfers' Beach** it is a magnificent expanse of sand, with huge breakers.

Gregory Town – the pineapple center of the island – is the next stop on the itinerary. The townsfolk still celebrate the Pineapple Festival every summer. They continue to harvest the fruit – admittedly in much smaller numbers – and distil a pleasing pineapple rum from it, which is known as 'Gregory Town Special'. No one should leave town without sampling this sweet spirit. Whether or not it is the pineapple rum which makes the people of Gregory so friendly is uncertain, but they are extremely hospitable.

About 5 miles (8km) further north, a single track of the Queen's Highway crosses Eleuthera's narrowest point via the ★ **Glass Window Bridge**. The vast expanse of glass-smooth waters below, where the deep blue of the Atlantic merges with the shimmering turquoise of Exuma Sound, gives it its name.

Glass Window Bridge

The inhabitants of the islets of Harbour Island and St George's Cay – better known as Spanish Wells – are none too happy to have their islands treated as simply a part of Eleuthera. Geographically they are not far away, but there are deeply-rooted historical reasons why the predominantly white and deeply religious St George's Cay islanders believe they should be treated differently.

That's life

★★★ **Harbour Island**, or 'Briland' as the inhabitants call it, was settled 300 years ago by Puritans. Towards the end of the 18th century, they were joined by Loyalists from the newly-independent USA. Before Nassau was established as the capital of the Bahamas, ★★★ **Dunmore Town** occupied this important role. This historic town, which can be reached by water-taxi from Eleuthera, should not be missed. The 3-mile (5km) long island with its powdery, pink beach and turquoise water has a truly inspirational atmosphere. The old, colonial-style clapboard cottages painted in pastel shades and surrounded by white wooden fences round off the picture. It also has the oldest Anglican church in the Bahamas, St John's.

Harbour Island beach

The 10-minute water-taxi crossing to ★★ **St George's Cay** leads into another world. The people of ★★ **Spanish Wells** – the name betrays the fact that Spanish vessels stopped off here to replenish their water supplies – are among the most prosperous on the Bahamas. They enjoy a reputation as the best fishermen for miles, specialising in that species of seafood which brings the richest rewards, the crawfish. The blond, blue-eyed inhabitants, all descendants of the Eleutheran Adventurers and Loyalists, form a white enclave on the Bahamas. This tightly-knit community of strict Anglicans and Methodists are said to be resented by the other islanders.

Clapboard house at Spanish Wells

You can hire a bike to tour the island, but there are no hire cars. It is a charming little place, with a number of churches and brightly-painted clapboard houses. There is also the Spanish Wells Museum, with artifacts from the time of the Eleutheran Adventurers.

Route 4

★ The Abacos

Tourist gem

Viewed from the air, the islands and cays of the Abaco archipelago look like a nibbled boomerang, although they are 124 miles (200km) long and 16 miles (25km) wide. The western half of Great Abaco consists of an inaccessible swamp that becomes a tattered net of many small islands. The tourist gems lie on the northeast side: Elbow Cay, Man-O-War Cay, Great Guana Cay, Treasure Cay and Green Turtle Cay. Walker's Cay, an angler's paradise, sits at the northern tip of the line of islands that fork off to the north of Little Abaco. The needs of every kind of tourist are catered for on the Abacos: tiny fishing villages New England-style, sailing and fishing

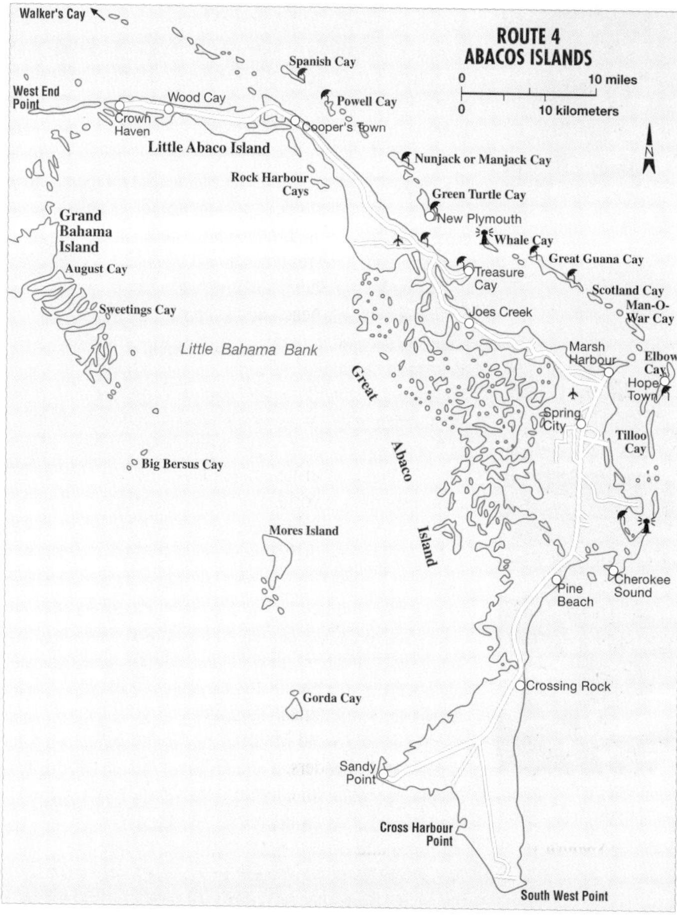

ROUTE 4
ABACOS ISLANDS
0 10 miles
0 10 kilometers
N
Walker's Cay
West End Point
Wood Cay
Crown Haven
Little Abaco Island
Spanish Cay
Powell Cay
Cooper's Town
Nunjack or Manjack Cay
Rock Harbour Cays
Green Turtle Cay
New Plymouth
Grand Bahama Island
Whale Cay
Great Guana Cay
August Cay
Treasure Cay
Scotland Cay
Man-O-War Cay
Sweetings Cay
Joes Creek
Little Bahama Bank
Marsh Harbour
Elbow Cay
Hope Town
Great Abaco Island
Spring City
Tilloo Cay
Big Bersus Cay
Mores Island
Cherokee Sound
Pine Beach
Crossing Rock
Gorda Cay
Sandy Point
Cross Harbour Point
South West Point

grounds that rank among the best in the world, many palm-ringed cays and even some urban pleasures in Marsh Harbour, the third-biggest town on the Bahamas. Last but not least, the lure of sunken treasure from the 500 or so boats that have foundered in the dangerous offshore waters over past centuries has proved irresistible for deep-sea divers.

Facing the future

History

Loyalists have dominated the history of these islands. They came in the 1780s from New York and North and South Carolina when they could not contemplate living in a country that was no longer loyal to the British crown. Their attempts to cultivate the barren land were ineffective, so they concentrated on the surrounding water. Many took to fishing, while others began building high-quality ships *(see page 41)*. There were some, however, who earned their living from wrecking. When the shallow waters caused a ship to run aground on reefs, the wreckers simply relieved it of its cargo. If the waters failed to ground enough vessels, some were lured from their course by flashing lights.

In comparison to many of the Out Islands, it is possible to get around here easily by car. A road – albeit in poor condition in places – runs from the southern tip of Great Abaco Island near the Hole-in-the Wall lighthouse to the northernmost point of Little Abaco Island. A boat, of course, is required for trips to the smaller islands. The island possesses several small airports, but tourists are most likely to arrive at the main town, **Marsh Harbour**. The town (pop. 3,500) is the business center for the islands and the main supply depot for tourists, sailors and locals, as it stocks fuel, food and all the other day-to-day needs. It is not just a supply point, however, but a holiday resort in its own right, with a large marina, a few hotels and some beautiful beaches.

Cracked conch and fries

Marsh Harbour makes a good base from which to explore the cays off the east coast or the north end of the island. The southern part of the 'boomerang' has little to offer tourists. Sandy Point and the area around Cooper's Town in the north are the only places on the west coast accessible by road. Few people venture out into the almost impenetrable swamps.

The Atlantic coast with its offshore island and beautiful beaches is the more attractive side. A full tour of the island can be tiring as the roads are very bad in places, the settlements are many miles apart, the endless pine forests can create a monotonous impression and even in the north of Great Abaco, there is little to see. Other than a few 'blue

holes' that the locals will have to point out, there are only two attractive spots: the modern tourist center of Treasure Cay and the sleepy village known as Cooper's Town.

By Out Island standards, ★★ **Treasure Cay** is a tourist haven, with a stunningly beautiful beach alongside the shimmering turquoise sea, an attractive golf course, a large marina, holiday homes, villas, a hotel, various restaurants and bars and a shopping center.

Treasure Cay

On the other hand, the little village of **Cooper's Town** further north belongs to a different world. Few visitors stray into the home town of the Bahamian prime minister Hubert Ingraham. Here – and also on the next-door island of Little Abaco – life revolves around the sea, the corner shop, the fuel station and the small churches and cafés.

To avoid long and tedious car journeys and to make the most of the more interesting cays off the east coast, it is best to start any trip in Marsh Harbour. A ferry that moors near the Great Abaco Beach Hotel takes visitors across to the little islands of Elbow Cay and Man-O-War Cay. Both islands are so small that they can be comfortably fitted into a day trip unless you want to spend a long time lazing around on one of them. These two, and Green Turtle Cay further north, make ideal bases for holidaymakers on longer stays who are seeking peace and quiet in a well-established community. However, Man-O-War Cay has neither a restaurant nor a hotel, so it is difficult to enjoy its isolated beaches in the evening.

Testing the water

To visit **Elbow Cay** with its main settlement of ★★ **Hope Town** is to enter a world untainted by development. A picturesque, red-and-white striped lighthouse greets new arrivals as they enter the tiny harbor. This frequently photographed navigational aid was built in 1830, but locals initially sought to sabotage it as it threatened their livelihood, bringing an end to the profitable trade of plundering ships that ran aground. From the top of the 120-ft (37-m) tower (Monday to Friday 10am–4pm) there is an excellent view of the sea and the neighboring cays.

A walk through the village (pop. 3,500) is an enchanting experience: brightly-painted clapboard houses, narrow, traffic-free streets and reserved but pleasant inhabitants. The majority of Hope Towners are descendants of Loyalist settlers. The concept of crime in this tightly-knit community is an alien one as everyone knows everyone else. Windows and doors are hardly ever locked at night.

Peace-loving and civilised are, ironically, the most appropriate adjectives to describe the ★★ **Man-O-War Cay** islanders. Many of the 170 or so inhabitants bear the surname Albury, a name almost synonymous with boatbuilding. This is another island which was settled by Loyalists in the 18th century and their descendants have a reputation for being even more disciplined and devout than on the neighboring islands. They are considered to be conscientious and honest people, regular church-goers; alcohol is banned and bikinis frowned upon. Visitors should, therefore, take care not to cause any offence to their hosts.

Peaceful New Plymouth

To reach the third, also very conservative, little island, it is first necessary to drive northwards for about an hour. The ferry to **Green Turtle Cay** departs from a harbor which lies a mile or two north of Treasure Cay. ★★ **New Plymouth**, the main settlement on the 3½-mile (5.5-km)

long and 875-yd (800-m) wide island strip, is also inhabited by the descendants of a colony of loyal English monarchists. The 400 islanders live in colorful clapboard houses and work as boatbuilders or fishermen, or in the tourist industry. There are a few pleasant restaurants, bars and a small museum in the town. The **Albert Lowe Museum**, housed in a 150-year-old building, contains models of Abaconian ships built by Albert Lowe, an early New Plymouth man, and other objects of historical interest. Life goes on quietly and peacefully with people moving around on foot, by boat or bike. The arrival of the weekly mailboat is an occasion for local gossip to be exchanged.

One of Albert Lowe's ships

With the boat considered the most important means of transport on the Bahamas, boatbuilding skills are highly prized. Since the invention of the aeroplane, the boatyards have had to come to terms with the competition it brings, but the boat is still as important a part of everyday life for most Bahamians as the car is for other nationalities.

Over the past 150 years Bahamian boatbuilders have earned a world-wide reputation as skilled craftsmen. There are two reasons for this: first, a boat was absolutely essential for getting about, for transporting goods and for fishing; and second, the islands had plentiful supplies of the right sort of timber.

At home in the harbor

The Abacos, and predominantly Man-O-War Cay, have been the center of the boatbuilding industry for as long as anyone can remember. The craftsmen here can make anything from a small, manoeuvrable dinghy to a large, cargo schooner. Outsiders may be forgiven for thinking that Man-O-War Cay is a peaceful backwater where time has stood still, but the boats that are built here can take on international competition.

Modern techniques, using glass fiber, are employed here and fast and stylish boats are produced in all sizes. Even so, there are still small concerns where experienced workers make boats from Bahamian wood in the traditional manner. Anyone who owns such a boat will treat it with the utmost care. And really it does not matter whether it is made of wood or fiber glass, if it bears the insignia 'Made in the Bahamas', then it is certainly something rather special.

Divers at Walker's Cay

Walker's Cay, the most northerly of all the Abacos islands can only be reached by hired boat or private plane. Walker's Cay Hotel and Marina was once a hide-out for pirates and other outlaws, but now it is mainly divers, mariners and deep-sea fishermen who use it as a base. In spring and summer, prestigious fishing competitions are held here. The nearby barrier reef attracts divers, but there is little else of interest on the island.

Great Exuma

Excursions to Other islands

★ The Exumas

Exuma Cays from the air

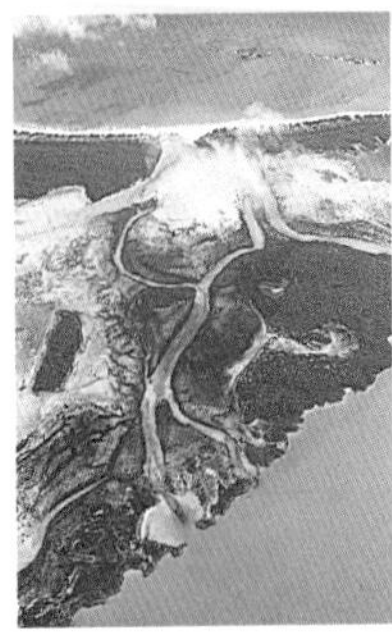

Like a string of pearls, the sandy cays of the Exumas extend for more than 100 miles (160km) through shimmering shades of blue and green. The hilly Exuma Islands are surrounded in the west by the crystal clear waters of the Exuma Bank and to the east by the Exuma Sound that plunges to a depth of 4,920ft (1,500m).

The total number of islands varies, depending who you talk to, but most islanders insist there is at least one island for every day of the year. It is true that from a tourist point of view the Exumas are not as well developed as, say, the Abacos or Eleuthera, but these small islands have more to offer those holidaymakers seeking peace and natural beauty than any other group of Bahamian islands. Most of the inhabitants live on one of the two larger islands, Great Exuma or Little Exuma, which are linked by an old, single-track bridge. Perhaps as a result of their isolation, the tiny islands in the north have become havens for fauna and flora.

History

It will quickly become apparent that almost all the inhabitants of the Exumas bear the surname Rolle. This harks back to the former plantation owner Lord John Rolle, who bequeathed not only his name to his slaves, as was the normal practice at the time, but also his extensive estates. The consequences of this act of great generosity are still felt today. Lord Rolle's land transfer documents have never been found so the precise circumstances regarding land ownership have become quite difficult to untangle. Here, on Great Exuma you will find settlements called **Rolleville**

Family tombs at Rolleville

and **Rolle Town**, originally two of the first of five plantations owned by the Rolle family. However, it does seem that the islanders are not that bothered about changing their comfortable and peaceful lifestyle. The greatest challenge today is negotiating the huge potholes on the island's aging roads, but it is hoped that this situation will soon improve, as plans are in hand for the roads to be resurfaced. Making use of produce from their own gardens or from the sea, the islanders are generally self-sufficient and many of them pick up a few dollars servicing the tourist industry.

Rolleville view

George Town is the islands' biggest settlement, but the fact that it is also an administrative center is certainly not apparent. The most impressive edifice in the little town is the pink-washed **Government House**, built in colonial style with imposing white columns. It houses not just the police headquarters, but also the offices of the government representatives, the courthouse and the prison. Only about a hundred yards away, the pretty Anglican **Church of St Andrew** stands on a hill. The view from here encompasses George Town itself and **Stocking Island**, which is noted for its beautiful beaches and **Mystery Cave**, an extensive system of underwater caverns.

Government House

By far the biggest attraction on the Exumas is the ★★★ **Exuma Cays Land and Sea Park** which covers an area of

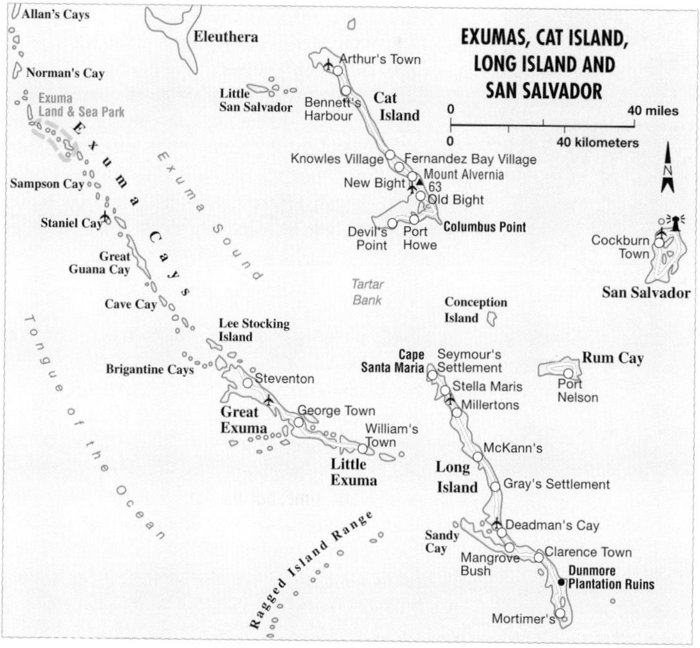

EXUMAS, CAT ISLAND, LONG ISLAND AND SAN SALVADOR

Allan's Cays
Norman's Cay
Exuma Land & Sea Park
Exuma Cays
Exuma Sound
Sampson Cay
Staniel Cay
Great Guana Cay
Cave Cay
Lee Stocking Island
Brigantine Cays
Steventon
Great Exuma
George Town
William's Town
Little Exuma
Tongue of the Ocean
Ragged Island Range
Eleuthera
Little San Salvador
Arthur's Town
Bennett's Harbour
Cat Island
Knowles Village
Fernandez Bay Village
Mount Alvernia 63
New Bight
Old Bight
Devil's Point
Port Howe
Columbus Point
Tartar Bank
Conception Island
Cockburn Town
San Salvador
Cape Santa Maria
Seymour's Settlement
Stella Maris
Millertons
Rum Cay
Port Nelson
McKann's
Long Island
Gray's Settlement
Deadman's Cay
Sandy Cay
Mangrove Bush
Clarence Town
Dunmore Plantation Ruins
Mortimer's
0 40 miles
0 40 kilometers
N

about 200sq miles (455sq km). It begins just north of Staniel Cay near Conch Cut and includes many tiny, uninhabited islands to the north as far as Wax Cay Cut. This nature reserve is a favorite haunt for divers and snorkelers as well as bird-lovers who can enjoy a guided nature walk here.

Naturalists are keeping a careful eye on **Allan's Cay** as it is the home of the threatened Bahamian iguana, which can grow to 3ft (90cm). The cost of visiting this park has to include the price of chartering a boat from one of the towns at the southern end of the Exumas, such as George Town (or else a speedboat from Nassau). For further information, either ask at one of the hotels or the Bahamas National Trust in Nassau (tel: 393-1317 or 393-2848).

The Regatta takes place in April

The Shark Lady welcomes visitors

The many unspoilt islands and the serenity of their inhabitants are two aspects of the Exumas which are appealing. For yachtsmen and women the added attraction is that the conditions here are ideal for their sport. Every April, the **Family Island Regatta** transforms the Exumas into something resembling a funfair, with the occasion ranking as the Out Islands' event of the year.

Travelers who are interested in the lives of the local people will discover that these islands have produced some extraordinary characters. One such example is Gloria Patience, a lady well over 70 years old, sometimes known as the 'Shark Lady'. This big-hearted and boisterous woman lives on Little Exuma in an old house through which, it is said, runs the **Tropic of Cancer**. Her living room serves both as a museum and a flea market. The Shark Lady tells of her adventures at sea and sells the exploits – any carcases – by stringing the bones together to make necklaces to sell to Exumas' visitors. Gloria claims to have taken care of about 2,000 specimens. The biggest was 18ft (5½m) in length, while the most memorable was a female hammerhead shark that tore her boat to shreds.

Long Island

It is not difficult to work out how Long Island got its name. At its narrowest point it measures only 4 miles (6km) wide but it extends for a distance of 62 miles (100km). Shortly after the arrival of the Spanish at the end of the 15th century, the Lucayans, the original settlers, were wiped out and Long Island was left uninhabited for many years. It was not until the 18th century that Loyalists from North and South Carolina (and their slaves) rediscovered the island. When the slaves were freed in 1834, the landowners departed and the cotton plantations declined. The freed slaves remained and their descendants make up most of the island's present population. Few people took any notice of Long Island until the 1960s when a group of German investors set about reviving the island's fortunes with a hotel complex.

Over 3,000 people now live on Long Island, earning their living from farming, fishing, salt production and low-key tourism. The small, but not insignificant contribution of tourism to the island's economy is largely focused on **Stella Maris**, a resort club in the north of the island. It is well known among the diving fraternity who come to watch sharks being fed.

The fierce-looking fish, which can measure up to 6ft (2m) in length, are attracted to the reef by regular food supplies. Amateur divers cannot resist the photo opportunities offered by the sharks, mainly Caribbean reef sharks and bull sharks *(carcharhinus leucas)* which enjoy the shallow waters close to land. Occasionally, one of the feared hammerhead sharks emerges from the deeper water. Although they are reckoned to be among the most aggressive of the species, no accidents have occurred as yet.

Residents of Shark Reef

As soon as the boat from Stella Maris arrives at ⋆ **Shark Reef** the first dark fins appear, gliding through the clear water. The group of divers – usually between six and 14 in number – are advised about the correct procedure. One after the other they quietly slip beneath the surface of the water and take up their agreed positions on the sandy sea bed. Backs against the reef and underwater cameras at the ready, the divers wait at least as expectantly as the hungry sharks for the fish-filled bucket to descend. The fish are not thrown into the water one at a time – as is the practice at other shark-feeding sites – but lowered into the water in one go. The 12 to 18 sharks have just one thing in mind, the struggle for food. The resulting film footage makes dramatic viewing.

Fine sandy beaches and shallow bays along the west coast contrast with the gently sloping hills in the interior and with the steep cliffs on the more rugged east coast. ⋆⋆ **Cape Santa Maria** is without doubt the finest beach on the island. It is situated at the northern tip of the island and its beauty lies not just in its incredibly fine white sand and turquoise-blue sea, but also in its sheer size and emptiness.

Evidence of the earlier white settlers can be found close to the villages in the shape of ruins which were once plantation houses on the cotton plantations. The most notable ones are at **Adderley's Plantation** near Cape Santa Maria, **Gray's Plantation** near Gray's Settlement and **Dunmore Plantation** south of Clarence Town.

Some of the unusual features on the island include metal spikes on the roof gables and trees that are decorated with bottles, sticks, bones and tufts of cotton. These fetishes are associated with the Obeah cult which has had considerable influence on the Long Islanders (*see page 59–60*).

Two churches in Clarence Town – one Anglican (St Paul's) and one Roman Catholic (St Peter's) – are symbols for the Christian faith and both were built by John Hawes, a priest well known throughout the Bahamas. Hawes, alias Father Jerome, came to the island at the beginning of the 20th century as an Anglican and later converted to the Catholic faith.

Agave, Cat Island

Cat Island

The sixth largest island on the Bahamas resembles a fish hook. It is noted not just for **Mount Alvernia**, at 206ft (63m) the highest peak in the Bahamian archipelago, but also for many tales of strange happenings: ethereal figures who guard buried gold treasure and Obeah spirits who can subject humans to the power of evil if they do not know how to appease them.

The most interesting sight on the island, the ★★ **Hermitage** on the summit of Mount Alvernia, can be approached from New Bight. This small, delightful chapel with a bell-tower and tiny rooms was built by Father Jerome *(see page 48)*. He spent the last years of his life within the confines of its low walls. He died in 1956, surrounded by a mystique that has given him a special place in the hearts of many Bahamians.

Christian beliefs and the occult coexist side by side on Cat Island. Many of the simple houses are decorated with Obeah symbols and objects which the inhabitants hope will keep evil spirits away. The islanders who are involved in Obeah are unlikely to speak openly about it for fear of antagonising the spirits, but with a little luck and

Breaktime

patience it is sometimes possible to hear one or two stories about supernatural occurrences and the rites practiced by the Obeah cult followers (*see page 59*).

Not quite so shrouded in mystery, but equally controversial, is the question of whether it was Cat Island – named after the pirate Arthur Catt – or San Salvador where Columbus and his men first landed in 1492. Names have been changed in the past and this has confused historians. On some maps Cat Island is called San Salvador and San Salvador becomes Watling's Island. However, in the official history of the Bahamas, San Salvador is cited as the place where Columbus first set foot in the New World. Despite this, the Cat Islanders have sought to immortalize the great explorer. The southeastern tip of the island points towards Spain and was therefore named **Columbus Point**. While this peninsula can only be reached on foot, the ruins of the Richman Hill-Newfield plantation near Devil's Point and the decaying mansion of the once-grand Deveaux cotton plantation near Port Howe are accessible by car.

Basketware for sale

It is difficult for tourists to get lost on this attractive island, but it is also quite difficult to get around, other than on foot, as the infrastructure is poorly developed. The roads – at least those that are tarred – are badly potholed. One or two hotels are situated in the south of the island but they are generally chosen by those in search of peace and seclusion. The waters off Cat Island are regarded as excellent for fishing and ★ **Fernandez Bay**, a part of the Fernandez Bay Village holiday center, has one of the finest beaches anywhere in the Bahamas. Casuarina trees offer shade and the cream-colored, sandy beach, shaped in an arc in true picture postcard style, slopes gently down into the warm turquoise sea.

Cat Island is home to about 2,000 people, most of them concentrated in Arthur's Town and **Bennett's Harbour** in the poorer north and **New Bight** in the south, at the foot of Mt Alvernia. Cat Island is the birthplace of the celebrated black actor Sidney Poitier, best known for his roles in films such as *Lilies of the Field*, *Guess Who's Coming To Dinner* and *In the Heat of the Night*.

San Salvador

Situated at the eastern end of the archipelago and over 186 miles (300km) from Nassau, this island with its 500 inhabitants only covers an area of about 68sq.miles (190sq.km). Nevertheless, it is the island with the greatest historical pedigree, in fact one of the most important in the New World, for it was here, according to most historians, that Christopher Columbus first set foot on dry land on October 12, 1492, after an eventful Atlantic crossing. It is true that some historians now question the validity of this account and conclude that the honor should be bestowed upon either Cat Island (*see page 46*) or Samana Cay, some 62 miles (100km) to the south east. But on the 500th anniversary of this significant event, the Bahamian government declared that it *was* on San Salvador that the Spanish explorer first landed.

Monument to Columbus

The actual spot is said to be about 3 miles (5km) south of **Cockburn Town**, the island's current administrative center. In 1956 a ★ **Monument** was erected at the spot where Columbus and his men are believed to have landed. When the momentous event's 500th anniversary was commemorated in 1992, an **Indian village** was built, enabling visitors to examine in detail the sort of huts in which the Lucayans lived. In Fernandez Bay an underwater monument has been placed at the spot where Columbus's boat first anchored.

In the northeast of the island, which is dotted with saltwater lakes, stands ★ **Dixon Hill Lighthouse**, the last lighthouse on the Bahamas where the beacon is a kerosene lamp. If a booking is made in advance the lighthouse keeper will arrange for visitors to look around.

Dixon Hill Lighthouse

As with so many other places in the Bahamas, it is not the island itself, but the turquoise waters off the coast which have most appeal. Whatever the time of year, divers and snorkelers can see through the crystal clear waters to a depth of about 200ft (60m). Long before anyone took an interest in San Salvador because of the Columbus connection, the international diving community once met in Riding Rock Inn, about half a mile (1km) north of Cockburn Town.

The runway at Cockburn Town's tiny airport is something of a curiosity: it crosses the town's main road, known as the Queen's Highway. In true Bahamian style, it is the planes that have priority.

Gray Angel fish

Andros

The wild and untamed island of Andros covers an area of 2,280sq miles (6,000sqkm) and as such is the biggest island in the Bahamas archipelago. It is also the largest unexplored area in the western hemisphere, making it a paradise for botanists, ornithologists, divers and adventurers. To look at the map this largely flat island resembles a jigsaw puzzle. The geography presents a difficult task for explorers as a network of inlets and lakes criss-cross the island. The main settlements are situated on the east coast: Nicholl's Town in the north, Andros Town in the middle and Congo Town in the south, but none of these places has more than 500 inhabitants. The impenetrable swamp along the western edge of Andros is uninhabited and is referred to as The Mud by the islanders.

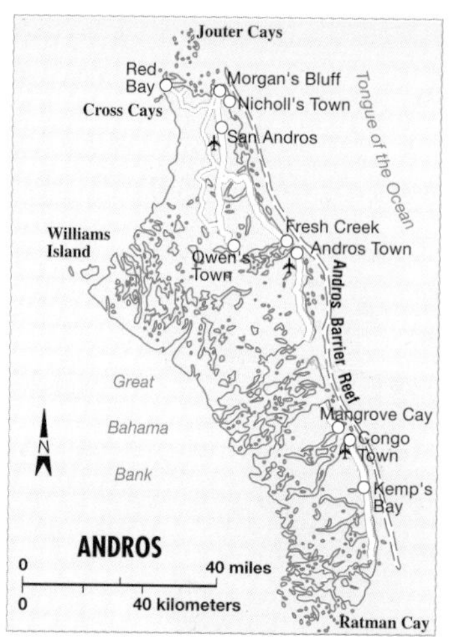

Trying to get around the island by car is tiresome as there are so many obstacles. Anyone wishing to travel from the north to the south will at the very least have to ask a local to guide them across the North Bight. However, most visitors do not come to Andros to attempt overland expeditions. The main attraction lies beneath the water a few hundred yards from the east coast. The ★★ **Andros Barrier Reef** which extends for 140 miles (225km) is the second longest barrier reef in the world – only Australia's Great Barrier Reef is longer – and must rank as one of the great adventures for divers and snorkelers. Because of a geological quirk, underwater explorers can have a glimpse of not just the small, colorful fish and corals which make their homes in and around the reef, but also those impressive sea creatures who dwell at lower levels, such as sea perch, barracudas, tuna and hammerhead sharks.

Beyond the unusual black, coral-covered rocky projection known as 'Over the Wall', which runs 45yds (40m) from the coast, lies the 6,000-ft (1,800-m) deep **Tongue of the Ocean** channel discovered 30 years ago. The diversity of the fauna and flora that exists at the lower levels of this mysterious trench have yet to be fully researched.

In amongst the coral

But, even on land, mystery still surrounds La Isla del Espiritu Santo (Island of the Holy Spirit) as the Spanish christened the island. Rumors abound of strange beings, such as the bird-like 'chickcharnies' who have sparkling red eyes and three-toed feet and who inhabit the dense forest in the island's interior.

The tourists are coming

Nonetheless, changing times have not entirely passed Andros and its 8,000 inhabitants by. Tourist numbers continue to rise and this has helped to increase the turnover at the small textile firm in Fresh Creek which produces Androsia batik.

Bimini Islands

The Compleat Angler Hotel

The tiny Biminis have a special appeal for Americans – they are only 50 miles (80km) from Miami. The author Ernest Hemingway was attracted to them for this reason in the 1930s, but what was more important to him was that a fishing expedition in the waters around the Bimini Islands was almost bound to provide magnificent sport. Many of today's visitors spend their time on the Hemingway trail, and are likely to spend as much time in his favorite bar at **The Compleat Angler Hotel** in **Alice Town** as they are deep-sea fishing. This is quite fitting, for the great man, whose alcohol consumption became legendary, spent a great deal of time here himself. For those who can tear themselves away, however, the main town on the island can offer everything that a dedicated fisherman could want: marinas, fishing tackle, accommodation and simple bars where the day's catch can be celebrated with a drink. Every year the dozen or so billfish tournaments draw numerous fishing enthusiasts to the islands (billfish are relatives of the swordfish).

Hemingway discovered the Bahamas in 1935. He lived in Florida's Key West and when he learned that the waters around the tiny Bimini Islands were ideal for sea angling he decided to check them out. For Hemingway, a writer who was increasingly attracted to the primitive and to man's strugggle against nature, the challenge of pulling in huge fish from the ocean depths became an obsession – one which he later wrote about memorably in *The Old Man and the Sea* (1952).

The two islands of **South Bimini** and **North Bimini** with a total area of only 9sq miles (23sq km) have three other big attractions. As with almost every other island in the Bahamas, water plays a prominent part: sailing, sunbathing and diving. Yacht owners appreciate the area as there are several well-protected bays between the two islands and also a relatively high number of marinas. The beautiful sandy beaches northeast of Alice Town are much favored by sun-worshippers, while beneath the water near **Paradise Point** on North Bimini lies a bizarre, rectangular rock formation that some explorers have claimed are the ruins of the lost city of Atlantis.

Most of the land on the Bimini Islands is either privately owned or swamp, so the majority of the 1,600 or so inhabitants live on a narrow strip in the east of North Bimini. There is no need for a car as the journey from Alice Town to the center of the second-largest settlement, **Bailey Town**, only takes about 10 minutes on foot. A Methodist church here dating from the middle of the 19th century is worth a quick look.

South Bimini has a few holiday homes and an airport. Several small cays lie off the southern coast. The best-known is **Cat Cay**, which is the location of the Cat Cay Yacht Club, an exclusive members-only club frequented by wealthy businessmen, the aristocracy and celebrities.

Berry Islands

The 30 or so little islands that make up the Berry Islands lie in an arc like a new moon about 37 miles (60km) northwest of New Providence. Most of the Berries are uninhabited, but some wealthy outsiders, such as Wallace Groves, the multimillionaire and founder of Freeport on Grand Bahama, have created their own little piece of paradise there.

The first settlers on the Berry Islands were liberated slaves who were brought to Great Stirrup Cay. The current number of islanders stands at 600 and most of these make their living from fishing, sponge diving and tourism. The main settlement is on **Great Harbour Cay** which is about 19 miles (30km) long and 1½ miles (2.5km) wide. **Bullock's Harbour** is a sleepy little spot with a few restaurants and a corner shop. Early in the 1990s a hurricane almost destroyed one of the two holiday resorts, the **Chub Cay Club** in the south of the Cay. The Berries follow closely behind the Biminis as a center for anglers, with sea perch, swordfish, mackerel, tuna and bonefish among the most sought-after species.

Sponges provide a living

Bird in paradise

Mayaguana Island

This Atlantic island approximately 108sq miles (300sq km) in area seems a world apart from the island capital of Nassau. Even the most adventurous tourists rarely make it as far as Mayaguana, an unspoilt natural paradise with some marvellous beaches. About 400 people have made their home on the island and most of these are fishermen and farmers who value seclusion.

The mailboat from Nassau, the *MV Windward Express*, having already stopped off on Crooked and Acklins Island

and on Long Cay ends its journey on Mayaguana. Privately chartered planes serve the island and there is a scheduled service by Bahamasair.

Determined travelers who make the journey will find a few beds in private guesthouses, but pre-booking is not an option because there are scarcely any phones.

Bahamasair has scheduled flights

Salt brings prosperity

Inagua

Great Inagua, the southernmost of all the islands, is also the third-biggest in the archipelago. On clear days Cuba can be seen from the southwest of the island and Haiti is nearer than Nassau. This flat island, about 56 miles (90km) long and just over 19 miles (30km) wide, is home to about 1,000 people. Rain is a rare occurrence, but a strong trade wind often blows. These inhospitable conditions, while not conducive to plant life, have enabled the islanders to enjoy a degree of prosperity from harvesting salt. The Morton Salt Company uses modern machinery to collect huge quantities of this essential mineral.

The scanty road network does not extend much beyond **Matthew Town** at the western tip of the island. The remainder of Great Inagua – and all of Little Inagua – is given over to the animals. Every year, in spring, thousands of flamingos gather on **Lake Windsor** (or Lake Rosa as it is called on many maps), thereby creating one of the biggest flamingo breeding grounds in the western hemisphere. Visitors to Inagua will soon appreciate that the bright pink flamingo does not appear on the Bahamian coat of arms by accident. It is believed that between 30,000 and 50,000 of the birds gather here each year. These beautiful creatures, which can reach a height of 4ft 6in (1.5m), will entertain birdwatchers with their springtime courtship displays, but later in the season they become preoccupied with caring for their young. Their mud nests are conical in shape and will usually contain two white eggs 2–4 inches (5–9cm) long. Many people are unaware that their bright colored plumage is not entirely natural: they acquire it by eating a special type of seaweed which they dig out of the mud with their beaks.

Lake Windsor

Keen to encourage and conserve these unusual creatures the conservationists of the Bahamas National Trust have established the ★★ **Inagua National Park**, with an area of 285sq miles (750sq km), covering more than a third of the whole island. Such intervention was necessary because these colorful birds, which used to be found all over the Bahamas, were under threat. Their tender flesh became a delicacy, and as their vivid plumage made them very visible targets and their trusting natures meant that they did not view man as an enemy, something had to be done to

protect them. The authorities will arrange accommodation and guided tours of the park. In fact, the only way this waterfowl paradise, which is also home to cormorants, pelicans and spoonbills, can be visited is as part of a conducted tour. Contact the Bahamas National Trust for details *(see Flora and Fauna, page 72)*.

Anyone who has seen a flock of flamingos emerging from the shallow water and setting off into the sun like a flying pink carpet, will undoubtedly confirm that making the long trip to Inagua is well worth the effort.

The uninhabited island of **Little Inagua** is another haven for birds, including West Indian tree ducks. This rare species does have to share the land with wild goats and donkeys, but they coexist in perfect harmony.

Acklins and Crooked Island

These two islands, linked by a ferry that runs between Lovely Bay on Acklins Island, and Browns on Crooked Island, together with **Long Cay** form a protective barrier for the **Bight of Acklins**, a shallow lagoon where a rare species of iguana *(anolis)* still survives on a number of the tiny cays.

Tourists are something of a rarity on the two islands which lie 225 miles (360km) from the capital, Nassau. Some 400 inhabitants earn their living from fishing and farming and very little disturbs their peaceful existence.

The islands played a significant part in the history of the Bahamas. On the coast of Acklins Island, archaeologists discovered the remains of a Lucayan settlement, possibly the largest in the Bahamian group *(see page 13)*.

Apart from the unspoilt natural environment typical of all the southern islands, there is little else to see on Acklins and Crooked Island other than some magnificent beaches, the remains of derelict cotton plantations and three 100-year-old lighthouses.

Flamingos on the lake

Watchful heron

Iguana anolis

Art and Architecture

Opposite: Junkanoo art

A casual visitor to Nassau might think that the culture of the Bahamas consisted of Las Vegas-style casino shows and the occasional play, operatic performance or orchestral concert. In reality it is much more: it is the Junkanoo tradition and Goombay music; the straw-plait designs produced by the women on the Out Islands; the Bahamian clapboard house and the mysterious, ever-present Obeah rites that are still practiced on the more remote islands.

Arts and crafts

The most widely practiced handicraft on the Bahamas is straw weaving. The items produced range from baskets, hats and purses to matting and dolls. The Out Islands, and Long Island in particular, are said to produce the best-quality products. The baskets are so tightly and carefully woven that they can even be used to carry water for short distances. There are a number of straw markets in the tourist centers of Nassau, Freeport and Lucaya where most of these souvenirs can be bought. On the Out Islands themselves it is possible to watch the weavers at work and, in most cases, the prices are lower.

Straw woven goods

There are a few renowned local artists: Mal Flanders and Macmillan Hughes, for example, who live on Eleuthera (*see page 34*). Many foreign artists and writers have settled on the islands at various times, the best known being the Nobel-prize winning author Ernest Hemingway who lived on the Bimini Islands for some time (*see page 50*). The islands' most famous son is probably Sidney Poitier, a distinguished actor and film director who made his name in Hollywood during the 1970s; he is a native Bahamian from Cat Island.

Ernest Hemingway

Architecture

Climate, geographical position and history have contributed to the development of a unique architectural style. The finest examples are to be found in historic Dunmore Town on Harbour Island in the north of Eleuthera and also in neighboring Spanish Wells. Other sites include New Plymouth on Green Turtle Cay just off Great Abaco and Hope Town on Elbow Cay. The Bahamian clapboard house is built in such a way as to allow a gentle breeze from the Trade Winds to blow in through the oversized windows. High ceilings increase the airflow to create an electricity-free, ecologically-sound kind of air-conditioning. A shutter above the window can be adjusted to create shade or to provide protection against tropical downpours and storms. To improve air circulation during the hot, damp summer months and also to raise the joists in

Clapboard house

The clapboard house, built to withstand the storms

case of flooding, a clapboard house stands on low wooden or brick supports. The wall boards are painted in bright colors, but they are not nailed down, just wedged in place. What initially sounds a rather fragile construction, turns out, because of its flexibility, to be extremely stable and one capable of withstanding the sort of violent tropical storms that would reduce conventional structures to rubble in a matter of seconds.

Painting by Albert Lowe

Historical New Providence

New Providence is steeped in history and the interested visitor should leave time to discover some of the beautiful buildings which line the streets.

Government House, Nassau, is the official residence of the Governor-General, representative of the British monarch. The pink and white neoclassical mansion house built around 1801 offers a wonderful view of the island.

Queen Street in Nassau features several buildings of note: Devonshire House, No 11, is considered by some to be a good example of early British colonial architecture, No 28 sports traditional dormer windows and ornate lattice work, and No 30 is a colonial-style, two-story structure with the ground floor made out of cut squared stone and the first floor of wood.

Nassau is home to an important historical archive, the Bahamas Historical Society Museum, set up in 1959. The building is also the society's headquarters. The small museum displays artifacts, works of art, photographs, maps and documents some dating from before Columbus. There is also a collection of Lucayan and Arawak Indian artifacts, jewelry and sketches. The colorful pirate tradition of the islands is depicted through paintings and prints. Look out for pictures of infamous mischief-makers like Edward Teach, alias Blackbeard.

Music and Dance

No celebration on the Bahamas is as loud, as colorful or as cheerful as Junkanoo, a festival that is often compared with the Carnival in Rio or the Mardi Gras in New Orleans. This extravaganza, one of the most important events in the Bahamian cultural calendar, originates from the years of slavery, when white colonists ruled the islands and the black people were worked to exhaustion on the plantations. Holidays in those days were rare and the slaves took full advantage of a few free hours during the days between Christmas and the New Year to really let their hair down.

The highlight of Junkanoo is on Boxing Day but the first few hours of the New Year are also important, when street parties are held and extravagant processions wind through the towns.

How Junkanoo received its name is not entirely clear. Many people believe it is derived from a slave called John Canoe, who had been an African chieftain before his capture, while others insist that Junkanoo is a corruption of the French expression *gens inconnus*, meaning unknown persons or masked figures. What is certain is that early Junkanoo festivities had strong parallels with African tribal rites and so it is assumed that its roots lie in Africa, probably with the Yoruba people, ancestors of many Bahamian slaves. One common Yoruba ritual features masked dancers, enacting an African form of ancestor worship. According to Yoruba culture, man owes his existence to the immortality of the human soul and every mask symbolises the spirit of a dead ancestor who is brought back to life by the dancing.

Junkanoo time

The designs and vibrant colors on the masks and costumes of early Junkanoo festivals showed great similarities with the clothes worn by earlier African dancers, who dressed from head to toe in vividly dyed materials. In the early Bahamian version, dancers wore colorful and imaginative costumes made of frilled paper or fabric, but instead of masks, they simply painted intricate designs on to their faces.

Today, Junkanoo dancers dress up in many different guises. There are stilt dancers, clowns and Obeah spirits, all with lively musical accompaniment provided by pipes, horns, empty conch shells, Goombay drums made from goatskin stretched over a wooden frame, and Bahamian cow-bells. The sound they create is characterized by shrill, deep and deafeningly loud tones, a distinctive combination which is now often portrayed as the national music of the Bahamas. Whereas in the past the shrill tones of Junkanoo were reserved for the carnival itself, over the past 50 years it has become the one of the typical sounds of the islands and can be heard at any time.

The king of the festival

Junkanoo exhibits

In line with the long tradition, the Junkanoo celebrations continue to take place around Christmas. Even those visitors who would rather spend public holidays in the comfort of their own hotel than on Nassau's brightly decorated Bay Street should not miss out on the opportunity to experience a Junkanoo. Visitors to the tourist centers of Nassau and Freeport at other times of the year can enjoy 'mini-Junkanoos' organized by the hotels. Like all such tourist-oriented tastes of local cultures, they lack authenticity, but nevertheless they are still great fun, and give some idea of what the real thing at Christmas and the New Year is like.

For some years now, a special Junkanoo exhibition – Junkanoo Expo – has been open in the converted customs warehouse on Prince George Wharf by Nassau harbor *(see page 19 & 22)*. Costumes, processional vehicles and musical instruments are on display, together with an explanation of the history of Junkanoo. There is also a smaller Junkanoo exhibition in the Grand Bahama Museum in Lucaya (*see page 32*).

The second typically Bahamian tradition that will be visible – and audible – to visitors is Goombay, with its gentle, rolling rhythms. Goombay is a fusion of three musical traditions: the music of the Bahamian people's African forebears, the music of the early American settlers, and that of the British colonial rulers. Originally, Goombay was produced by a range of large, specially made goatskin drums, but now more modern instruments such as pianos, saxophones and guitars provide the melody, with rhythmic accompaniment by bongo drums, maracas and rhythm sticks. The distinctive sound of Goombay has now spread to other tropical islands such as Bermuda, but its traditional home is in the Bahamas.

Rake 'n' scrape

Obeah

Obeah is part of the Bahamas cultural heritage. This mysterious form of spiritualism is strongest on the Out Islands, particularly Cat Island, and has its roots in African religious beliefs, overlaid with European superstitions and elements of the Christian faith. Similarities with Haitian voodoo, the Santería of Cuba and the Shango of Trinidad have often been highlighted.

The remote location of the Out Islands and the often turbulent mixture of cultures have proved to be a fertile breeding ground for supernatural beliefs. Talk to the islanders about Obeah and they will either laugh and dismiss it as mumbo jumbo or else pretend that it does not exist.

Not surprisingly, then, visitors will find it difficult to learn much about Obeah. It is rarely mentioned in front of outsiders and certainly never discussed by anyone who believes in, and fears, the sinister forces.

Any visitor who does wish to find out more about Obeah rites should look to Cat Island, Andros or Long Island. Symbols marked on the houses of the local people bear witness to belief in the spirit world. In order to deter evil spirits, Obeah believers attach sharp metal spikes to the rooftops of their huts. Other fetishes include empty bottles, bones and glasses, while decorated trees in front gardens indicate the homes of Obeah practitioners. When the parents of believers die, the rest of the family must leave their home and build another one directly alongside. In that way, contact with the spirit of the deceased is avoided.

Obeah tree

With a little patience it is possible to win the trust of a believer and persuade him or her to recount an Obeah story. One word of warning: fact and fiction are often difficult to tell apart when woven into a story or tall tale. Magical rituals are performed by Obeah men and women and outsiders would be unlikely to witness such an event without the assistance of a local. Comparisons are often made between Obeah sorcerers and Indian medicine men. Certainly the application of Bahamian bush medicine is a significant part of their work but it has little to do with mysticism and much more to do with a thorough knowledge of the healing properties of plants.

More extraordinary, however, is the ability of Obeah devotees to put themselves into a trance, a state which apparently facilitates contact and conversation with the spirits. Obeah masters believe they can bring about good or evil, make people rich, poor, ill or healthy and release them from a spell. Both forms of magic can be employed for 'fixing' a person with a spell – or worse – 'cursing'. The less serious 'fixing' can be lifted by any Obeah practitioner with the required knowledge, but a 'curse' can only be lifted by the one who cast it.

Snake or witch?

Obeah masters or witches are said to appear in animal form – for example, as a rat or a snake. A small, fat snake with a tie round its body is particularly feared, as the ribbon is a sure sign that the reptile is a witch in disguise. Even to the sophisticate who has no time for superstition, Obeah can seem very real on the islands.

Island medicine

Some plants can cure

Jumbay, cerasee, strongback, lifeleaf, soldier vine or love vine are the names of just some of the 50 plants which are found in the medicine chest of every Bahamian family. Before islanders think of going to a doctor, they will often try out some of the natural bush remedies. There is a herb for every minor complaint and, of course, on the remote islands many people have no choice but to rely on self-diagnosis and treatment. Knowledge about the healing powers of the various plants has been passed down from generation to generation.

If anyone complains of an ailment, one of the men or women in the family will investigate the medicines available, collect plants and prepare infusions or compresses. Even in sophisticated Nassau the first-choice remedy for flu is cerasee tea, augmented with a little salt and lemon juice which lend a bitter aroma.

Cerasee is a quick-growing vine with bright yellow flowers and orange seeds. Soldier vine creeps along the ground almost unnoticed, but – as the name suggests – it is said to bring renewed vigor to fighting men. Bread fruit was brought to the Caribbean from the Pacific Islands by Captain Bligh of *Mutiny on the Bounty* fame. It is usually taken to relieve high blood pressure and headaches. Seaside morning glory or bay hop can be found in plentiful supply by the beaches and is used to treat gynaecological complaints.

Festivals

January About three hours before dawn on New Year's Day, the Junkanoo Festival begins with street processions, music, masked dancers. Best viewed in Nassau, although celebrations take place throughout the islands.

Ready for the Regatta

April The Family Island Regatta is the most important annual sailing event in the Bahamas. It takes place in George Town on the Exumas and attracts countless Bahamians and tourists as well as sailors, and turns the Exumas into a fairground with Skipper parties and Junkanoo parades.

June The Goombay Summer Festival lasts from June to October and introduces tourists to Goombay and Junkanoo music. Events run right through the summer on the main tourist islands. Information from the Bahamas Tourist Office (*see page 85–6*).

July Independence Week is celebrated everywhere on the islands. July 10 is Independence Day, marking liberation from British colonial rule in 1973. Parades and fireworks enliven the big day.

Independence Day fireworks

August First Monday in the month, the Fox Hill Festival in Nassau begins. This is a celebration of the emancipation of the slaves in 1834, and includes junkanoo among the festive events.

October October 12 is Discovery Day, commemorating the moment when Christopher Columbus first set foot on the islands. San Salvador is the best place to enjoy the celebrations.

November November 5, Guy Fawkes Day, demonstrates the Bahamas' close ties with Britain and its history. At night during the street parade a dummy of Guy Fawkes is hanged and then finally burned.

December Junkanoo celebrations start early on Boxing Day with parades and street dancing. The party starts up again on New Year's Day. Best viewed in Nassau.

Junkanoo celebrations

CAFÉ
BANANAS

Tropical
Cocktail
Specials

Food and Drink

Opposite: tropical tastes

Bahamian cuisine reflects the wide cultural roots of the islanders. Elements have been borrowed from the Caribbean, the United States, Britain and other European countries and then mixed together with traditional Bahamian products. Thus a distinctive repertoire has emerged in which the firm, white flesh of the conch undisputedly plays a primary role.

Conch chowder and cracked conch

The conch (pronounced 'konk') is an important ingredient in most Bahamian dishes. The inside of this impressively large shellfish, whose pinky shell makes a popular tourist souvenir and is also used as a musical instrument by the local people, tastes rather bland and can be quite chewy, but a skilled Bahamian chef can soon change that. The conch is usually liberally spiced and can be served as a snack, as part of a salad, as the main ingredient of a soup, as an hors d'oeuvre or as a main course.

Conch salad

Conch chowder is a delicious fish soup made from finely chopped conch flesh and then garnished with an imaginative combination of potatoes, vegetables, ham and spices. Another favorite of the islanders is conch salad. Raw pieces of conch are prepared and served with a hot and sour marinade, strips of pepper and onion slices. Cracked conch is a main course made with breaded conch fillet and served with a selection of vegetables. Those who find the thought of mussel flesh unappetizing ought at least to try conch fritters. These traditional Bahamian croquettes conceal relatively small quantities of the meat.

After conch, it will probably be grouper. This delicious fish, which resembles cod, can be prepared in a number of ways. Probably the most popular is with slices of almond. Another local delicacy comes from the warm coastal waters: catching crawfish or spiny lobster is one of the main occupations on Spanish Wells. The flesh of this creature is highly prized, and is only available fresh from April to August. Crabmeat, bonefish and snapper are other fish frequently found on the menus of local restaurants.

Red meat has to be imported, so it is no surprise that many Bahamian dishes are developed from locally reared chicken. The richly-flavored flesh is often served with spicy peas and rice or johnnycakes, plain fritters which can be dunked into the gravy.

Guava duff is one of the Bahamas' best known desserts but it is a recipe which requires a lot of time to prepare. It is made with guava pulp and a cinnamon cream.

When choosing an evening meal, whether it is a romantic candlelit dinner in a top-quality hotel or a cheap and cheerful family supper in a simple country restaurant, it is worth bearing in mind that Bahamians, particularly on the Out Islands, usually eat at around 8pm. While in Nassau and the main tourist centers many restaurants stay open until much later, in the quieter areas restaurateurs usually like to close by 9.30pm.

Try the local liquor

Rum is usually associated with Cuba and Jamaica, but it has for a long time been a favorite drink among Bahamians. Inventive bartenders have devised a number of popular cocktails such as Yellow Bird (banana liqueur, rum, apricot brandy, Galliano, orange and pineapple juice), Bahama Mama (rum, créme de cassis, grenadine, lemon juice and a pinch of nutmeg) and Goombay Smash (coconut rum and pure rum, Triple Sec, a little syrup, pineapple and lemon juice). Many bars have their own variations of these well-known favorites. Treat them with respect – some of them pack quite a punch.

...or an imported alternative

If downing too many rum cocktails or New Providence Kalik beers the night before has left you with a sore head, then the tried and tested breakfast cure for a hangover consists of conch in a marinade of lemon sauce, butter, onion and hot, red peppers. Conventional Bahamian breakfasts have much in common with the traditional American version: scrambled or fried eggs with bacon, ham or sausage, pancakes with syrup or jam, toast with butter and marmalade, followed by fresh fruit – melon, strawberries and kiwis. A variety of pastries such as croissants, muffins, doughnuts and cheese puffs may be available. Then there is coffee, tea and several varieties of freshly squeezed fruit juices, which are available in many different guises throughout the day.

Restaurant selection

The following suggestions for some of the most popular spots in the Bahamas are divided into three price categories: **$$$** = expensive, **$$** = moderate, **$** = inexpensive.

Seafood stall in Nassau

Nassau
$$$Buena Vista, corner Delancy and Meeting Street, tel: 322-2811. Continental cuisine. 200-year-old villa in colonial style. **$$$Graycliff**, West Hill Street, tel: 322-2796. Continental cuisine in historic building. One of the best known – and most expensive – restaurants in Nassau. Reservations necessary. **$$$Sun And ...**, Lake View Road near Shirley Street, tel: 393-1205. The most delightful restaurant in Nassau and a popular meeting place. Difficult to find, so a taxi recommended. French cuisine. Reser-

vations, jacket and tie essential. Closed in August and September. **$$Green Shutters Restaurant**, 48 Parliament Street, tel: 325-5702. Favorite with anglophiles. Country pub atmosphere. English/Bahamian cuisine. **$$The Poop Deck**, East Bay Street, tel: 393-8175. Seafood restaurant eight minutes drive from the city center. Large terrace by the water's edge. Fine view of Paradise Island. **$Europe**, in Ocean Spray Hotel on West Bay Street, tel: 322-8032. German specialties served. **$Roselawn Café**, Bank Lane near Bay Street, tel: 325-1018. A delightful restaurant in the heart of the old town. Pretty terrace. Italian/Bahamian cuisine. **$Bahamian Kitchen**, Trinity Place near Market Street, tel: 325-0702. One of the most popular places for traditional Bahamian fare.

Cable Beach

$$$Le Café de Paris, on West Bay Street in Le Meridien Royal Bahamian Hotel. The most romantic of all the restaurants in Cable Beach with an aristocratic feel. Superb French/Bahamian cuisine. **$$$Androsia Seafood Restaurant** on West Bay Street in the Henrea Carlette Hotel, tel: 327-7805. Nautical feel to this German-run restaurant. Haunt of film stars. Reservations recommended. **$$Round House Restaurant**, West Bay Street in Casuarinas Hotel, tel: 327-8153. Family-run restaurant with highly-acclaimed Bahamian/American cuisine.

Crystal Palace resort, Cable Beach

Paradise Island gardens

Paradise Island

$$$Bahamian Club, Bird Cage Walk opposite the Atlantis-Paradise Island Resort, tel: 363-3000. Continental cuisine served in a smart, Georgian-style dining room. Reservations and jacket for dinner essential. **$$$Café Martinique** in Atlantis-Paradise Island Resort, tel: 363-3000. Excellent, exquisitely decorated French restaurant with view of lagoon. Reservations and jacket for dinner essential. **$$$Courtyard Terrace** in Ocean Club Hotel, tel: 363-3000. Romantic spot for a dinner for two – located in the middle of a tropical palm garden. Reservations and jacket for dinner essential. **$$$Coyaba**, in casino complex of Atlantis-Paradise Island, tel: 363-3000. Very good Chinese food. **$$Villa d'Este** on Bird Cage Walk in Atlantis-Paradise Island Hotel, tel: 363-3000. Elegant Italian restaurant. Reservations essential.

Freeport

$$Ruby Swiss, near the Bahamas Princess Tower, tel: 352-8507. Swiss-managed restaurant offering continental cuisine with a wide menu. **$$Guanahani's Restaurant** in the Hotel Princess Country Club, tel: 352-6721. Barbecue and seafood. Romantic atmosphere. **$$Pier 1**, Freeport Harbour, tel: 352-6674. By the cruise ship harbor.

Lucaya

$$Luciano's, in Port Lucaya, tel: 373-9100. One of the best Italian restaurants on Grand Bahama. **$$The Stoned Crab**, by Taino Beach, tel: 373-1442. Excellent seafood dishes in large portions, by the beach. **$Pusser's Co. Store and Pub**, Port Lucaya, tel: 373-8450. Popular meeting place with magnificent view over the marina. Simple continental and Bahamian cuisine.

Pause for claws

Eleuthera

$$$The Cove, in The Cove Eleuthera Hotel. Delicious, Bahamian/American cuisine in a tropical-style restaurant.

Harbour Island/Dunmore Town (Eleuthera)

$$$Runaway Hill Club in hotel of same name in Dunmore Town, Colebrook Street. Bahamian/American cuisine with magnificent view of pink sands. **$$Angela's Starfish Restaurant**, corner of Dunmore and Grant Street in Dunmore Town. Popular for its simple, economical, but delicious Bahamian cooking. **$$Coral Sands Mediterranean Café** in hotel of same name. Dinner only by prior reservation. Very good fish dishes served on terrace with view over palm garden and sea.

Harbour Island restaurant

Marsh Harbour

$$Harbour Lights, in Great Abaco Beach Hotel, tel: 367-2158. Bahamian and international cuisine, with beach view. **$$Mangoes Restaurant**, Front Street. Specialises in Bahamian dishes. A popular meeting place for mariners and locals. **$$Wally's**, Bay Street, tel: 367-2074. Casually elegant dining, live entertainment in the evening.

Elbow Cay/Hope Town (Abacos)

$$$Club Soleil, Western Harbourfront, by the marina. Bahamian seafood a specialty. **$$Harbour's Edge**, popular with the locals, Bahamian menu.

Green Turtle Cay/New Plymouth (Abacos)

$$New Plymouth Inn in hotel of same name. Delicious Bahamian dishes in relaxed but romantic atmosphere.

New Plymouth Inn

The Exumas

$$Sam's Place, Main Street, George Town. First-rate Bahamian cuisine. Meeting place for yachting fans. Most of the hotel restaurants and bars can also be recommended.

Bimini Islands

$$Fisherman's Wharf, King's Highway, Alice Town, in the Bimini Fishing Club, tel: 347-3391. Best food on the Biminis. **$$Anchorage Dining Room**, Kings Highway, Alice Town. Terrific view over the harbor.

Nightlife

Nightlife in the Bahamas is to be found mainly in the capital, Nassau. When night falls over the old town and the adjoining districts of Cable Beach and Paradise Island, the tired horses that have pulled the surreys around the hot streets of Nassau all day start to nod off. At the same time, the city's night spots begin to come to life with the neon-lit casinos, reminiscent of Las Vegas or Atlantic City, attracting the first customers. Entrance is free, but a bit of pocket money is required. Even non-gamblers find the atmosphere exciting, and there is usually a cabaret or stage show running at the same time in the complexes.

Crystal Palace Casino

Casino and cabaret
The Palace Theatre, Carnival's Crystal Palace Resort and Casino, Nassau, tel: 327-6200. Glamorous and glitzy, remember to book. **Le Cabaret**, Paradise Island Casino, tel: 363-2222. Cocktail and dinner shows every night. **Casino Royale**, Princess Casino, Freeport, tel: 352-7811. Cabaret includes can-can dancers.

Caribbean and North American discos
Club Waterloo, East Bay Street, tel: 393-1108. Caribbean music, Monday to Saturday, 11pm–4am. **Fanta-Z**, West Bay Street in the Marriott Hotel, tel: 327-6200. Disco every night, 9pm–4am. **Rock and Roll Café**, next to the Nassau Beach Hotel in Cable Beach, tel: 327-7711. Loud rock music, daily, noon–1am. **Le Paon**, Sheraton Grand Hotel on Paradise Island, tel: 363-2011. Large, modern disco. Friday and Saturday, 9pm–2am.

Calypso
Coconuts, East Bay Street, Nassau, tel: 325-2148. Live music on Friday and Saturday night. **Pick-a-Dilly**, Parliament Hotel, Parliament Street, Nassau, tel: 322-2836. Live music every night.

Jazz
The Vintage Club, Buena Vista Restaurant, Nassau, tel: 322-2811. Contemporary jazz. **Café de Paris**, Le Meridien Royal Bahamian, West Bay Street, Nassau, tel: 327-6400. Holds an enjoyable Sunday jazz brunch.

There are also numerous other bars and small clubs where you can hear calypso music and a number of junkanoo music venues. Check the local newspapers for details of what's on, or buy the useful publication called *What to Do*.

For security reasons, take a taxi home after a night in the bars, discos or casinos. Majestic Tours offer a good – and safe – tour of Nassau's bars, tel: 322-2606.

Bahamian blues

Local pottery

Shopping

It is easier than you would think to shop 'til you drop in Nassau. For one thing, the heat makes it difficult to keep a cool head and then the duty-free prices are always very tempting. Bay Street is the shopper's paradise, it offers the best selection of stores with shelves piled high with products bearing internationally-known names.

Shrewd shoppers are often on the hunt for other bargains soon after they arrive. Armed with a list of prices back home – or perhaps just a good memory – and a comfortable pair of shoes, they set to work. Whether it is clocks and watches from Switzerland, cameras from Japan, Parisian perfume, crystal glass and linen from Ireland or porcelain from Britain and Germany, prices actually differ very little from shop to shop, but it is worth taking a stroll down the side streets of Bay Street. The shops here often have special offers or sell finished lines. Caution is required with jewelry, clocks and watches. It is advisable to stick to the major outlets as a trademark or an authentic-looking certificate are not always the guarantee of a genuine product in the Caribbean. Reputable traders, on the other hand, cannot afford to be found selling counterfeit goods. Look for pink flamingo signs in shop windows, which means that the establishment is accredited by the government as a vendor of authentic goods. The International Bazaar and the Port Lucaya Marketplace on Grand Bahama can also be a heavenly shopping haven.

International jewelry...

...and watches

Watches and jewelry

Cartier has an exclusive outlet on Bay Street, Nassau, carrying a variety of upscale accessories including jewelry, watches and sunglasses. Also with a showroom on Bay Street is **Gold and Diamonds**. The company manufactures a wide range of silver and gold goods locally. All jewelry is duty-free. Paradise Towers Casino, Paradise Island ,is home to **Paradise Jewels** which sells semi-precious stones. The **Tick-Tock Shop**, on Bay and Market Streets, Nassau, offers a variety of watches and clocks with modern, funky designs.

Perfume

A comprehensive line of US and French cosmetics and perfume can be found at the **Beauty Spot**, Bay Street, Nassau. Classic scents are also on sale at the **Perfume Bar** on Paradise Island. **The Perfume Factory** at the International Bazaar, Freeport, creates unique fragrances from flowers, herbs and fruits found on the islands.

Crystal and china

Several stores carry well-known lines of crystal such as Waterford and fine bone china. For a good selection check out **Little Switzerland** on Bay Street, Nassau, **Midnight Sun** at the International Bazaar, Freeport and **Francis Peek**, George Street, Nassau.

Leather goods

The **Brass and Leather Shop**, Charlotte Street, Nassau stocks shoes, bags, belts and more besides. While **Fendi Boutique**, Bay and Charlotte Streets, Nassau imports the genuine designer articles from Italy.

Cameras

Brand-name photographic equipment and cameras are sometimes sold at discount prices at **John Bull**, in Nassau, Freeport and Paradise Island.

Paintings

There are some very interesting galleries in and around Bay Street, Nassau, where you can find some fascinating paintings by local artists.

If you are looking for something a little more ethnic and representative of the islands to take home, your first stop will probably be the famous **Straw Market** where the narrow lanes are piled high with hand-made produce. The women greet the passers-by with a 'Hello, sweetheart. I've got a nice straw hat for you.' Only the range of T-shirts exceeds the variety of straw products in this lively shopping area. Most of the islands have a straw market, selling the baskets, hats, table mats, etc. for which the Bahamas are well known, as well as hand-crafted conch and coral jewelry and locally made liqueurs. There is usually less variety on the smaller Out Islands, but keep an eye open for gifts sold by vendors at the roadside.

Popular logos

Conches for sale

Bougainvillaea

Fauna and Flora

Naturalists – and the tourist industry – generally appreciate that in ecological terms the Bahamas is still in relatively good shape. This is not the consequence of a highly developed environmental awareness, but has more to do with a collection of circumstances which have helped to preserve the islands in their original state. One important factor is that only 30 of the islands are inhabited, and, with a few exceptions such as Grand Bahama, there is practically no industry to speak of.

While most Bahamians are unaware of the need for environmental protection, such as the protection of endangered animals and plant species, the government is becoming increasingly aware of the need to preserve Bahamas' reputation as a modern Garden of Eden. Government ministers realize that it is not just the near-perfect climate that attracts tourists to the Bahamas, it is also the unspoilt natural beauty of the islands.

Life under water

Creatures of the deep

The range of fauna and flora underwater among the numerous reefs is extraordinary. Divers and snorkelers will see some amazing sights amid the Andros Barrier Reef which, at 140 miles (225km) long, is the second-longest barrier reef in the world *(see page 49)*. But, even in the other reefs which extend for more than 1,450 miles (2,330km), there is a multitude of brightly-colored sea creatures, including the spotted moray eel, the clown fish, the yellowtail, the parrot fish, trigger fish and trumpet fish, the goat fish, the wrasse, the reef perch, mackerel, kingfish and the small four-eyed butterfly fish, whose second pair of eyes are 'painted' on its rear side.

Mammals

The number of mammals on the Bahamas is not so impressive. Apart from the domesticated animals which were imported by the early settlers and which have been allowed to roam in the wild, such as pigs, donkeys and horses (Abaco), there are only 13 other species. Twelve of them are varieties of bats and the thirteenth is the **hutia** or **capromys**, a rodent that is unique to the islands. It looks like a cross between a rat and a rabbit and is seen in large numbers on the tiny East Plana Cays, and the Exumas Cays Land and Sea Park. A number of whale and dolphin species, such as the blue whale, humpback whale and spotted dolphin, also swim in the waters around the islands.

The hutia is unique to the islands

An osprey leaves its nest

Birds

Bird species are far more plentiful. About 230 types of birds live or overwinter on the islands and some are very rare, including the threatened Bahamian parrot (Abaco and Inagua), the Bahamian hummingbird, the Bahamian swallow, the West Indian swallow, the West Indian flamingo (Inagua), the great blue heron, the barn owl, the peregrine falcon and the Bahama duck.

A lizard lounges

Reptiles

Several interesting species of reptiles lurk by the seashore or amid the rocks and undergrowth on the islands. The 44 recorded species include a number of rare sea turtles. Altogether there are 27 varieties of lizards and 10 different kinds of snake. Not all are poisonous, although the Bahamian boa constrictor can be dangerous, depending on its size and the size of its prey.

Iguanas are the most fascinating of the islands' reptiles. The Bahamian people, who admittedly have a healthy interest in the mystical world, describe the iguanas as 'Bahamian dragons'. But these descendants of prehistoric beasts do not breathe fire. Four hundred species of iguanas still exist in the world but many are threatened with extinction. Four types of *anolis* (iguana) live on the Bahamas. It used to be a common sight to find them lazing on the beaches, but the local people regarded these primitive-looking creatures primarily as a source of meat and so their numbers have dwindled.

The smaller varieties of iguana live on the cays in the Bight of Acklins Lagoon between Crooked and Acklins Island, and on San Salvador they are extremely timid. Larger iguanas live on Andros and the northern Exumas. Rock iguanas *(cyclura inornata)* are the most unusual of the Bahamian species; growing to about 3ft (90cm) and weighing over 26lbs (12kg). This iguana can only be found on Allan's Cay, north of the Exuma National Park. Their dignified stature and trusting nature fascinate visitors.

There is something about these reptiles that is reminiscent of the dragon. They have a dull yellowy skin covered with a zigzag pattern and also have reddish shadows around their heads and the top of their legs. The rock iguana's deep red eyes also invite comparisons with prehistoric monsters, yet the creature is a peaceable herbivore and attacks man only if it feels threatened. The rock iguana's reputation has perhaps suffered because some of its relatives on the American mainland, such as the black iguana, can be aggressive and will certainly bite anyone who gets too close.

Sea grape tree

Plants

Of the 1,370 plant species to be found on the islands, about 120 are unique to the Bahamas. Among the most common are the Bahamian pine, the mahogany tree, the white, red and black mangrove, various orchids, guana berries, bay geranie and sea grapes. A number of Bahamian hardwood trees and some orchids have had to be placed on the list of threatened species.

Protecting the parks

National parks

In order to preserve the fauna and flora both on land and at sea, the **Bahamas National Trust** (BNT), a non-profit making organisation, has been set up and is charged with the task of protecting the natural environment. It is funded by donations, membership subscriptions and government aid. The BNT controls over 400,000 acres (160,000ha) of land in 11 national parks and nature reserves.

Exuma Cays Land and Sea Park is responsible for protecting unique plants and animals, such as the rock iguana and the strange-looking hutia. **Inagua National Park** is one of the biggest flamingo reserves in the western hemisphere. **Conception Island Park** is an important breeding and overwintering ground for flocks of birds. Turtles also breed close to the shore. **Lucayan National Park** on Grand Bahama contains one of the oldest underwater cave systems. **Retreat** on New Providence, a garden with a broad range of palms, is the headquarters of the BNT. The Bahamian conservationists also supervise **Peterson Cay Park** off Grand Bahama, **Pelican Cays Land and Sea Park** (Abaco) and other reservations such as the **Black Sound Cay National Reserve**, a tiny mangrove island in Black Sound off Green Turtle Cay (Abaco).

Two nature reserves of particular interest to plant lovers are the 100-acre (40-ha) **Rand Memorial Nature Centre** in Freeport, and the **Garden of the Groves** (12 acres/5ha) in nearby Lucaya, which is a riot of tropical color. Contact: *The Bahamas National Trust, PO Box N-4105, Nassau, tel: 393-1317 or 393-2848.*

The Best Beaches

Gently washed by clear water and bordered by palms, many of the sandy beaches of the Bahama Islands are almost perfect. Some of the best are described here.

Fernandez Bay on Cat Island: a delightful little bay with a fine sandy beach that runs down gently to the sea. Take idleness to its limits and relax with a long cool refreshing drink in a hammock beneath the casuarina trees of Fernandez Bay Village.

Harbour Island (Dunmore Town) off Eleuthera: some 3 miles (5km) of pink sandy beach washed by a sparkling sea of turquoise.

Treasure Cay Beach on Great Abaco Island: a 4-mile (6-km) long, half-moon shaped beach with dazzlingly white sand just one of the reasons why it is popular all year round. Fine view over the offshore cays and the sleek yachts passing by.

Cape Santa María on Long Island: offers a treat to visitors seeking peace and solitude, with miles of isolated, stunning white sandy beach and clear seawater at the northwest tip of the island.

Other beautiful beaches: **Love** and **Saunders Beach** in the north and **South Beach** in the south of New Providence; **Paradise Beach** on Paradise Island, a lively private beach shaded by casuarina trees; **Gold Rock Beach** and **Pelican Point** on Grand Bahama; **Great Harbour Cay**, a part of the Berry Islands (great mussels); **Stocking Island** off George Town on Great Exuma with a beautiful beach and the Mysterious Cave, accessible only to divers; and the vast secluded nature reserve of **Exuma Cays Land and Sea Park**, covering around 200 sq miles (500 sq km) of land on the Exumas.

Long Island Beach

Treasure Cay Beach

Great Exuma Beach

Perfect for watersports

Active Vacations

The Bahamian archipelago is a haven for outdoor enthusiasts. On land there are numerous opportunities to appreciate the local flora and fauna, as well as indulging in a variety of sports, while the surrounding waters will enthuse sea anglers, sailors, snorkelers and divers. The mysterious blue holes, the clear sea, the rich variety of fish, the stunningly beautiful coral reefs, the dramatic precipices and shallow bays are perfect for every type of watersport.

The hidden world of the reefs

Reefs

Reefs seem to hold a magnetic attraction for divers. Immersing themselves in a welter of colors and shapes that sway in the currents, they can swim among the fish and the other sea creatures that inhabit this hidden world. Divers are often also fascinated by the many sunken ships that litter seabeds close to the reefs. Reefs generally form in warm but shallow waters. Corals are the main visual feature, but many other organisms play an important role in creating this fantastic underwater scene. Algae comprise the main structure, but snails, molluscs, worms, echinoderms, and rhizopods all play their part. The ideal conditions for reef-forming organisms are plenty of light, warmth and clear, oxygen-rich water with little sediment.

A colorful resident

Of the different types of reef, there are **fringing reefs**, just offshore, **barrier reefs** which resemble fringing reefs but are generally much bigger and lie further from the coast, **platform reefs** which form where the sea bed is close to the water's surface, and **atolls**, rings surrounding a lagoon. The waters surrounding the Bahamas provide the ideal conditions for reef formation. Many different varieties of coral thrive here but the most impressive are probably the elkhorn *(acropora palmata)*, staghorn coral, seafans and honeycomb coral. The Andros Barrier Reef (*see page 49*) is one of the few places where striking black coral can be found.

Diving and snorkeling

As well as reefs, there are shipwrecks *(see below)* and caves to entice the diver into the water. The island of Andros with the second-largest barrier reef in the world and the Tongue of the Ocean, a dark and eerie gorge that plummets 5,900ft (1,800m) below the surface, is a diver's paradise. Chub Cay on the Berry Islands which lies at the northern tip of the Tongue of the Ocean is sometimes described as a 'fishbowl' as there are so many fish. Although all the Bimini Islands have a special place in the affections of sea anglers, the bizarre rock formations off Paradise Point (North Bimini) are a major attraction for divers. Some explorers claim that these are the remains of the sunken city of Atlantis. Divers will require nerves of steel if they are to sample the 'rollercoaster' at the northern tip of Eleuthera. A ride through the fierce currents of this underwater tunnel lasts about 10 minutes.

The diving's great

The northern **Exumas** can offer almost everything that a dedicated diver could wish for, from the world-famous Thunderbird Grotto, where Ian Fleming's James Bond survived a dangerous ordeal, to unexplored caves and mysterious deeps.

Grand Bahama, headquarters of the best-known Bahamian diving school, UNEXSO (*see page 30*), is noted not just for the Treasure Reef and its sunken gold treasures but also for one of the biggest underwater cave complexes in the world. The famous shark reef at Stella Maris *(see page 45)* on **Long Island** is another place for intrepid divers as it is possible to get a close view of sharks feeding. Finally, the small island of **San Salvador** deserves a mention. In fact, it is high on the list of priorities for most divers. At 50 different spots, underwater precipices drop to 40ft (12m), 100ft (30m) and 165ft (50m), offering insights into the fascinating world of underwater fauna and flora. Large sea perch and elegant rays, timid turtles and occasionally even a curious and brave shark will be among the passers-by.

Stella Maris resort

In search of sunken treasure

The waters around the Bahamas have sometimes been described as an underwater museum. Listed below are some of the most interesting and more easily accessible wrecks.

Some wrecks are accessible

Abaco Islands

USS Adirondack: the 125-year-old American warship with a few well-preserved cannons lies in only 20ft (6m) of water off Man-O-War Cay.

Andros

The Barge: about 30 years ago this old vessel was sunk in water only 65ft (20m) deep near Fresh Creek north of Andros Town. Now the coral-covered wreck is home to shoals of perch which always appear happy to be photographed by divers.

Bimini Islands

Sapona: the working life of the *Sapona* was spent transporting building materials and smuggling alcohol. During World War II it was used for target practice. Now it lies in 20ft (6m) of water off South Bimini and is a popular spot for night diving.

Eleuthera

Train Wreck: just 16ft (5m) below the surface of the water sits a ship that was sunk in 1865. It was carrying an unusual cargo, a locomotive, bound for Cuba. Only yards away from the wreck lie the rusting remains of the 200-ft (60-m) steam locomotive.

Grand Bahama

Theo's Wreck: this 230-ft (70-m) steel freighter was intentionally sunk off Freeport/Lucaya. The stern of the vessel lies close to the edge of a 2,000-ft (600-m) deep gorge.

Windsurfing

Long Island

Cape Santa María Ships' Graveyard: the *MS Comberbach* lies in 100ft (30m) of water off Cape Santa María. The wreck of a pleasure boat that sank in an accident also lies nearby.

San Salvador

The Frescate: this 265-ft (80-m) freighter ran aground and

Cable Beach

then sank to a depth of 20ft (6m). It is now a popular spot for novice divers.

Angling

Prize catch

Anglers reckon the waters surrounding the Bahamas have more fish than practically anywhere else in the world. Not only is there a wide range of edible fish and 'sport fish', but the islands can also provide boats for hire, chandlers and crew. The cost of a half-day fishing trip (including a boat for two to six people, equipment and crew) can vary. Those who thrive on competition and an audience, can take part in the many fishing competitions which are held throughout the year.

The Bimini Islands boast about being the 'Big-Game Fishing Capital of the World'. In the 1930s they had a champion for this point of view in Ernest Hemingway, himself a fanatical sea angler, who looked on the island as his adopted home for a while. Even today, records for some of the big catches such as sailfish, marlin and swordfish keep being bettered. **Walker's Cay**, north of the Abacos, is a small but very good center. In the holiday complex of the same name, everything revolves around angling as there are excellent opportunities in the coastal waters for deep-sea fishing, spear fishing and shoreline fishing.

The same is true of the tiny island of **Chub Cay** (Berry Islands). Sea perch, tuna and snapper are found here in huge numbers. Other good fishing grounds exist off **Cat Island** (which holds the world record for wahoo, a tasty fish that prefers to swim in the deep channels by the reefs), off **North Eleuthera** and **Andros**, the favorite waters for the bonefish.

This is the fish that many anglers regard as presenting the greatest challenge to their skills. It can usually be seen in clear, shallow waters. Extremely shy, but equipped with amazing vision and hearing, it will dart off at the slightest disturbance and is consequently very difficult to catch. Despite the bonefish's light weight (2–4lbs/900–1800g), it puts up a bitter struggle once hooked. Natural coral formations in every conceivable shape and color, sponges and other bizarre underwater plants also attract divers.

Delicate coral

Spiny Lobster

Before setting off in search of any sea creature, it is essential to check up on the regulations concerning seasons and quotas. Sponges and turtles may not be removed from the sea at all and the valuable Bahamian lobster can be caught only at certain times of the year and in certain quantities. Anglers and divers must remember that they are not allowed to put conch in an ice-box and bring it back with them when they come ashore.

For further information, contact the Bahamas Tourist

Office or the Department of Fisheries, PO Box N-3208, East Bay Street, Nassau, tel: 393-1777, fax: 393-1014.

Friendly shark

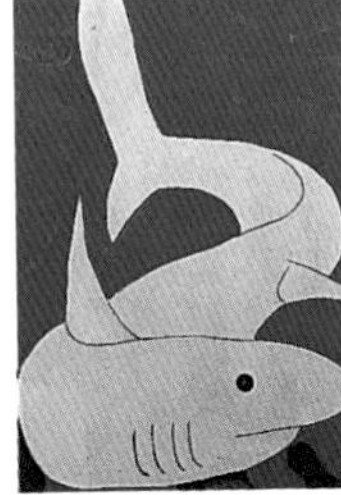

Fishing competitions

Long before tourism came to the Bahamas, amateur fishermen from all over the world saw the islands as the perfect place to practice their hobby and a number of small, family-run holiday complexes on the Out Islands have specialized in meeting the needs of fishing enthusiasts. Fishing competitions take place on most islands, with the best-known probably the **Bahamas Billfish Tournament**. This competition is spread over a period of five months and fishing takes place at a number of locations. Prey are exclusively fish that belong to the swordfish family.

The Bahamas Tourist Office or the Bahamas News Bureau, tel: 327-7678 can provide up-to-date information on fishing competitions. Tel: 305-923-8022 (USA) for details of the Bahamas Billfish Tournament.

Undesirable habits

Unfortunately, there are still many people who see nothing wrong in killing simply for sport. One of the most sought-after fish for deep-sea anglers is the blue marlin. This gleaming blue member of the swordfish family is a magnificent creature and it makes good sport for anglers because of its size and the tremendous fight it puts up when hooked. However, after the celebrations and the obligatory photo, the fish, which is bony and inedible, is simply thrown back into the sea.

Ready to launch

The fishing season

Allison tuna – June to August; amberjack – November to May; barracuda – all year; black fin tuna – May to September; blue fin tuna – 7 May to 15 June; sea perch – all year; kingfish – May to July; sailfish – summer and autumn; tarpon – all year; wahoo –January and February.

Sailing

Whether it is the high seas and adventure that appeal or simply anchoring off a dream island and relaxing, the Bahamas is the perfect place. Sailing enthusiasts rate it very highly, probably alongside the Virgin Islands and the Grenadines. The many tiny islands and peaceful bays, the crystal clear water, plus a comprehensive back-up network of marinas, repair yards and specialist suppliers, are just what sailors want. The Abacos are the most popular islands with the sailing fraternity, but other favorite spots are Cays Green, Turtle Cay, Man-O-War Cay and Elbow Cay (east of the Abacos), the Berry Islands, Eleuthera's Harbour Island and Spanish Wells, the Exumas and its countless cays. Boats can be hired on all the

larger islands – with or without crew (without crew is called bare boat). The Bahamas Tourist Office (*see page 85–6*) can supply the necessary information, but *The Yachtsman's Guide to the Bahamas* is an indispensable guide when planning a round trip. It is published by Tropic Isle Publishers, PO Box 610935, N. Miami, FL 33261-0935, USA, tel: 305-893-4277 and can be ordered by post. The regatta is to the sailor what the billfish tournament is to the angler. Races are organized all through the year, with the best-known being the **Family Island Regatta** held off the Exumas in April.

Children enjoy the Regatta, too

Golf

Devotees of golf will find a number of carefully tended greens on the Bahamas, some of which meet PGA standards. The Bahamas National Open is held on Grand Bahama where there are four courses: Bahamas Princess Hotel and Golf Club, two 18-hole courses, tel: 352-672; Fortune Hills Golf and Country Club, 9-hole course, tel: 373-4500; Lucaya Golf and Country Club, 18-hole course, tel: 373-1066. New Providence has three courses, each with 18 holes. The Cable Beach Golf Club, tel: 327-6000; South Ocean Beach Hotel and Golf Club, tel: 362-4391; Paradise Island Golf Club, tel: 363-3925. Both the Treasure Cay Golf Club on Treasure Cay (Abacos), tel: 367-2570 and Cotton Bay Club on Eleuthera, tel: 334-6156 have 18-hole courses.

Flying

There are opportunities for tourists to add a further exciting dimension to their holiday. A Cessna 172 or a Piper PA 28 plus an airfield on one of the small Out Islands are usually available for flying lessons. For further information, contact Stella Maris Resort Club, PO Box 30105, Long Island, tel: 338-2106.

ROYAL CARIBBEAN

Getting There

There are only two ways to get to the Bahamas: by plane or by boat. Although there are scheduled services for both, many flights and cruises form part of holiday packages. A few visitors make their own way to the Bahamas either by private yacht or motorboat.

By air

Visitors can fly direct from Miami and Fort Lauderdale, Florida, to the airports on Grand Bahama, Paradise Island and Eleuthera. Also Chalk International Airlines runs an amphibian plane service to the Bimini Islands from both Fort Lauderdale and Miami's Watson Airport.

There are two direct flights each week from London Heathrow to Nassau International Airport. Contact British Airways: for callers within the Greater London area, tel: 0181 897 4000; for callers outside the Greater London area but within Britain and Ireland, tel: Linkline 0345 222111. However, the vast majority of flights originate from airports within the United States, and therefore involve a stopover for visitors from Britain and the rest of Europe. Enquire at travel agents, as many of the large carriers make the trip, from over 20 different US airports. There are also flights from Canada and Jamaica.

By sea

Despite the ease and frequency of flights, the majority of tourists arrive by cruise ship. No other port in the Caribbean receives as many visitors as Nassau. Most of the cruise liners that moor in Nassau, Port Lucaya or Grand Bahama begin their journey in Florida, usually Miami, but some come from Port Canaveral and Fort Lauderdale. As well as the long Caribbean cruises in which the Bahamas are often the first or last port of call, cruises lasting between one and four days are also available.

Companies that serve the Bahamas include Carnival Cruise Lines, Miami, tel: 800-327-7373, Chandris and Celebrity Cruise Line, Miami, tel: 800-423-2100, Cunard Cruise Line, New York, tel: 800-221-4770, Dolphin Cruise Line, Miami, tel: 800-222-1003, Kloster and Norwegian Cruise Line, Coral Cables, tel: 800-327-7030, Majesty Cruise Line, Miami, tel: 800-532-7788, Premier Cruise Lines, Cape Canaveral, tel: 800-327-7113, Royal Caribbean Cruises, Miami, tel: 800-327-6700. (All the 800 numbers are toll-free when dialed from within the US).

In Europe cruises are usually booked through travel agents and these are generally all-in tours which can include flight, transfer and hotel accommodation. Holidaymakers already in Florida should look out for last-minute bargains at local agents specializing in Bahamas tours.

Opposite: arriving in style

Welcome to paradise

Most tourists arrive by ship

Getting Around

Island hopping

By air

Having reached Nassau, there are planes and boats to all the Out Islands (scheduled or chartered). Nearly all the islands that may interest tourists have a small airport. When flying to Eleuthera, remember that there are three airports: North Eleuthera, serving the north of the island, Governor's Harbour, serving the center, and Rock Sound, for the south. If you go to the wrong one it can cost you a small fortune in taxi fares. Andros also has three small airports. Flights to the Out Islands last on average between 40 and 90 minutes, but Inagua is a 2½-hour journey. The major airline company on the Bahamas is the state-owned Bahamasair which serves 19 airports on 12 islands.

Bahamasair, **US:** tel: 305-593-1910; fax: 305-477-1830. **UK:** tel: 0171 437 3542. **Bahamas:** tel: 322-4727.

A friendly greeting

Other companies that offer inter-island flights are Airways International between Abaco, Eleuthera, Exuma and Grand Bahama, tel: 305-887-2794; American Eagle linking New Providence, Grand Bahama, Abaco, Eleuthera and Exuma, tel: 800-433-7300; Chalk's International Airline, Bimini and Paradise Island, tel: 305-359-7980; Delta Connection Comair, New Providence and Grand Bahama, tel: 800-354-9822; Gulfstream Airlines, Eleuthera, Exuma, Abaco, Andros and Grand Bahama, tel: 305-871-1200; Island Express, Exuma, Eleuthera, Abaco, Long Island, Berry Islands, Andros and Bimini, tel: 305-359-0380; Taino Air Service, Grand Bahama, Abaco and Walker's Cay, tel: 352-8885; USAir Express, New Providence, Abaco and Eleuthera, tel: 327-8886. (NB: European readers should preface the above numbers with the 001 US dialing code.)

The following private charter companies serve the Out Islands: Air Link (Florida, tel: 407-283-1300), Congo Air (Nassau, tel: 377-5382), Miami Air Charter (Florida, tel: 305-251-9649), Pinder's Charter Service (Nassau, tel: 327-7320).

Island hopping

Ferries and mailboats

Island hopping by mailboat is an unconventional and adventurous way of getting around and fares are reasonable. Departing from Potter's Cay in Nassau, the 20 or so mailboats call at all the inhabited islands. For further information, consult the dockmaster, tel: 323-1064.

Chartered boats are more comfortable but much more expensive. They can be hired 'bare boat' or with crew.

Buses

Nassau and Freeport/Lucaya have 'jitneys', state-licensed buses. In Nassau these run a continuous service to Cable Beach and outlying areas between 6.30am–7.30pm. There is a bus service between Freeport and Lucaya, but there is no timetable. Nassau is the only place on the island which has 'surreys', or horse-drawn carriages. Otherwise use a boat, taxi, hired car or hired moped.

Jitneys and surreys

Car hire

Hire car companies on the island include Avis, Budget, Hertz, Dollar Rent-a-Car and National.

Nassau: Avis (tel: 377-7121), Budget (tel: 377-7405), Hertz (tel: 327-6866), National (tel: 377-7301).

Freeport: Avis (tel: 352-7666), Dollar Rent-a-Car (tel: 352-3714), Hertz (tel: 352-9250), National (tel: 352-9308).

On Cat Island, try Russell Brothers, tel: 354-5014; on Andros, Cecil Gaiter, tel: 329-3043, On Andros you are recommended to hire a car with a local driver, because the roads are so bad. On the other islands enquire at hotels for details of car rental, but be warned that on many of the smaller islands the roads are in poor condition and road signs are generally inadequate. Also, fuel is not always easy to come by on the Out Islands.

Drivers on the Out Islands are advised to acquire a copy of *Atlas of the Bahamas* before leaving Nassau. In the event of a breakdown or accident, drivers are on their own, as there is no emergency breakdown service in the European sense. Before touring any island, it is sensible to let someone know your destination and time of return. Remember to drive on the left. The speed limit in built-up areas is 25mph (40kph) and 40mph (65kph) outside towns.

Stretching out the ride

Taxis

Taxis use meters, and a nationally agreed structure applies to fares, so a visitor will know what to expect anywhere on the islands. Drivers will also negotiate fares on an hourly basis. A tip of about 15 percent is usual. In Nassau, water taxis operate between 9am–5.30pm, linking Prince George Wharf and Paradise Island. For further information enquire at hotels or the tourist information offices.

For guided tours of Eleuthera by taxi, contact either Maude Peterson, Governor's Harbour, tel: 332-2283 or Major's Taxi Service, Harbour Island, tel: 333-2043.

Bikes

Bikes are an excellent way of getting around the islands. Most of the Out Islands have bike hire outlets. In Nassau, try Bowes Scooter Rentals, Prince George's Wharf.

Getting to Know You

Visitors to the islands who wish to make closer contact with the Bahamian people and get to know more about the culture can do so through the increasingly popular **People-to-People** scheme which is supported by the tourist authority. This method of establishing personal links between tourists and locals was started in 1975 in Nassau and extended one year later to Freeport. In the meantime some of the Out Islands, such as Abaco, Exuma, Bimini and San Salvador, have joined the scheme. In Nassau there are over 1,000 volunteers and in Freeport about 400 who are very happy to spend time with tourists and to introduce them to the lively culture and way of life of the Bahamian people.

Meet the locals

The scheme, which is free to tourists, is arranged by the Ministry of Tourism. Before any personal contacts are made, the tourist must fill in a questionnaire and an evaluation of the answers helps the scheme's organizers to find a suitable match. Meetings are usually quite casual and are arranged to take place after 5pm or at the weekends as most of the volunteers are working people. Holidaymakers are expected to stay in hotels, not with their hosts. One highlight of the People-to-People scheme is the grand Tea Party in Government House (January to August on the last Friday of the month) when the participants are welcomed by the wife of the islands' Governor General.

The **Home-Away-from-Home** program is run by the same government department and provides host families for foreign students studying at colleges in the Bahamas, while the **People-to-People Weddings** scheme run by the tourist office is specifically for couples wishing to marry in a paradise island setting on the Bahamas. Another scheme will arrange pen friends. Anyone interested in the People-to-People scheme or in getting married under the Bahamian sun should contact their nearest Bahamas Tourist Office before they leave home *(see page 85)* or the relevant authority on the islands: The Manager, People-to-People, PO Box N-3701, Nassau, tel: 326-5371 or 326-9772, fax: 328-0945, or alternatively, The Co-ordinator, People-to-People, PO Box F-40251, Freeport, Grand Bahama, tel: 352-8044.

A **One-Stop-Shop-Agency** has been established in the Bahamas, enabling foreigners to raise business questions on a one-to-one basis. The agency is known as the Bahamas Investment Authority.

For more information, contact: Office of the Prime Minister, Cecil-Wallace-Whitfield Centre, West Bay Street, Cable Beach, PO Box CB 10980, Nassau, tel: 327-5970; fax: 327-5907.

Service with a smile

Facts for the Visitor

Travel documents

Visitors from the US, Britain, the former Commonwealth countries and Western Europe do not require a visa for stays of up to three months, although they must possess a valid passport – with the exception of US citizens who can sometimes get away with a birth certificate or driver's license. For further information contact the Bahamas Tourist Office (*see below*) or the Immigration Department, PO Box N-831, Nassau.

Jewelry is a popular souvenir

Customs

The amount of goods which may be taken out of the country varies somewhat depending on length of stay. Visitors from the USA have a higher duty-free allowance than others. If in any doubt, ask at your point of entry/exit. No one may take tortoiseshell products, coral, plants or fruit out of the country.

Pets

Pets must be over 6 months old and have a valid import permit. Contact the Director of Agriculture, Department of Agriculture, PO Box N-3028, Nassau for details.

Pets require a permit

Tourist information

US: Bahamas Tourist Office, 150 East 52nd Street, 28th Floor, New York, NY 10022, tel: 212-758 2777; 19495 Biscayne Blvd, Miami, FL 33180, tel: 305-932 0051.
UK: Bahamas Tourist Office, 3 The Billings, Walnut Tree Close, Guildford GU1 4UL, tel: 01483 448900
Bahamas: The Ministry of Tourism on the Bahamas is housed in the same building as the Straw Market: Ministry of Tourism, Bay Street, PO Box N-3701, Nassau, tel: 322-7500, fax: 328-0945.

Bahama dollars

Tourist information offices in Nassau are located in Bay Street, Rawson Square and at the airport (tel: 327-6806).

Bahamas National Trust, PO Box N-4105, Nassau, tel: 393-1317 or 393-2848.

On Grand Bahama the Ministry of Tourism has offices at the airport (tel: 352-2052), at the cruise harbor (tel: 352-7888), in the International Bazaar (tel: 352-6909) and in Port Lucaya (tel: 373-8988); the information office of the Grand Bahama Island Promotion Board is in the International Bazaar (tel: 352-7848).

How about an emerald?

Currency

The official currency is the Bahama dollar (B$) which is tied to the US dollar. Both currencies are accepted everywhere on the islands. All other currencies should be converted into dollars at banks in Nassau or Freeport/Lucaya or at their respective airports. Hotels will also change money but charge a higher commission than banks. Credit cards are generally accepted on New Providence and Grand Bahama, but on the Out Islands – apart from the main holiday centers and hotels – cash or US$ travelers' checks are recommended.

Tipping

Most restaurants include a service charge, but otherwise a tip of about 15 percent is normal. Taxi fares are usually rounded up, and hotel porters expect approximately 1$ per item of luggage.

Opening times

Businesses, government offices and shops: Monday to Friday, 9am–5pm or 6pm. Shops are usually open on Saturday.

Banks: Monday to Thursday, 9.30am–3pm, Friday, 9.30am–5pm.

Have card, will talk

Public holidays

The Bahamas has 10 national holidays: New Year's Day, Good Friday, Easter Monday, Whit Monday, Labor Day (1st Friday in June), Independence Day (10 July), Emancipation Day (1st Monday in August), Discovery Day (12 October), Christmas Day and Boxing Day (25 and 26 December).

Postal services

Post offices are open Monday to Friday, 8.30am–5.30pm and Saturday, 8.30am–12.30pm.

Telephone

The international dialing prefix for the Bahamas is 00 1 809. To call Britain from the Bahamas, dial 011 plus the area code and number. International calls made from the Bahamas can be very expensive, especially from hotels. Visitors would be well advised to use international telephone cards.

Time

Atlantic Standard Time now operates in the Bahamas (GMT less 5 hours, less 6 hours in summer).

Voltage

Mains voltage in the Bahamas is 110V, 60 cycles AC. An adapter, best purchased before traveling, is required for 220 volt appliances.

What to take

As well as swimming costumes and light clothing made from natural fibers, include a hat to protect against the sun, a water-resistant sun cream with a high protection factor, sun block for nose and lips and an insect repellent for the early morning and evening.

While casual wear is acceptable on the Out Islands, in Nassau's top restaurants, men are expected to wear a jacket and tie and women should wear a cocktail dress. Swimming costumes should only be worn on the beach or by the swimming pool.

Medical

Medical provision on the Bahamas is generally of a good standard. In the main population centers of Nassau and Freeport/Lucaya, visitors will have no difficulty finding a doctor or a hospital. On the Out Islands, there are currently 107 medical practices and smaller clinics. If the facilities on the Out Islands are not adequate, then an emergency air service will fly patients to the Princess Margaret Hospital in Nassau. In emergencies, tel: 919.

Medical provision is good

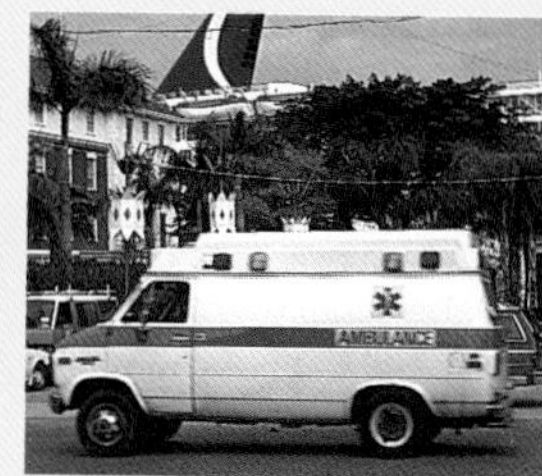

Any traveler requiring regular medication should bring a good supply with them. It is also a good idea to purchase over-the-counter remedies for headaches, toothache, sore throats and stomach disorders before setting out.

No health agreement exists between the UK and the Bahamas, so medical insurance is essential. In all cases medical costs have to be paid at the time of treatment.

No special inoculations are necessary for the Bahamas and the tap water on both the main islands is regarded as safe to drink, but bottled mineral water is obviously less risky. The biggest threat to the holidaymaker comes from the sun. Protective measures should be taken at all times.

Policemen are smart

Photography

Locals, even Straw Market traders, appreciate a polite request if you want to take a photograph of them.

Emergencies
Police, fire brigade and emergency air service: tel: 919
Ambulance in Nassau: tel: 322-2221.

Disabled visitors
There are about 30 hotels equipped for handicapped people. For further information consult a travel agent or the Bahamas Tourist Office(*see pages 85–6 for addresses in the US, London and the Bahamas*). There is also a Desk of the Disabled at the Ministry of Social Services in Nassau, tel: 323-3333.

Crime
On the Out Islands crime is not a problem but, with drug-taking prevalent in Nassau and in Freeport, it is safer not to venture too far outside the town center and the main tourist centers at night. Whenever possible, take a taxi.

Press and media
No fewer than six newspapers including two national daily newspapers (*The Nassau Guardian* and *The Tribune*) will keep visitors informed. Kiosks sell US and British newspapers. *What's On in Nassau* is a another useful tourist guide. There are several radio stations on the islands, a TV station and many US satellite TV stations broadcast programs to Bahamian homes and hotels.

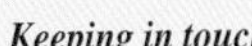

Keeping in touch

Diplomatic representation
Canada: Out Island Traders Building, Nassau, tel: 393-2123 during office hours or 393-2124 after hours.
USA: Queen Street, PO Box N-8197, Nassau, tel: 322-1181 during office hours.
United Kingdom: Bitco Building, East Street, Nassau, tel: 325-7471 for emergencies and 323-4286 after hours.

Watery grave for drug runners

Accommodation

The lap of luxury

For travelers to the Bahamas, the choice of accommodation ranges from luxury resort with casino and golf course to private holiday villa to simple Bahamian guest house. New Providence with Cable Beach and Paradise Island have 72 hotels and guesthouses which can offer a total of 7,764 rooms. On Grand Bahama there are about 3,000 rooms. Even the Out Islands have over 2,000 rooms.

A word of warning is necessary. Accommodation categories do not correspond with European or American standards. Hotels classified as 'Deluxe' or 'First Class' may not meet all expectations. Try to find out as much as possible about the hotel's facilities before departure. Travel agents, the Bahamas Tourist Offices abroad and the tourist information offices in Nassau and Freeport (*see pages 85–6*) will provide relevant information. A tax of about 8 percent should be added to all overnight accommodation prices. On Cable Beach and Paradise Island, an additional surcharge of 2 percent is payable.

Resorts

The major holiday complexes are usually situated by the sea and have their own sandy beaches, swimming pools, restaurants, bars and sports facilities.

British Colonial Beach Resort

Hotels

The dividing line between a resort and a large hotel is sometimes difficult to define. Given the same facilities and level of comfort, hotel prices will not differ greatly from resort prices. In both, you should expect to pay about 20 percent more in winter, when demand is greater.

Holiday flats and homes

In self-catering accommodation a maid service can be requested as an extra. People who do not like the hustle and bustle of a hotel and want to live like Bahamians will feel more comfortable in a holiday apartment. However, this type of accommodation is not usually included in many holiday brochures.

The US agents listed here specialize in self-catering accommodation: Condo World, 4230 Orchard Lake Road, Suite 3, Orchard Lake, MI 48323, USA, tel: 313-683-0202; Hideaways International, PO Box 4433, Portsmith, NH 03802-4433, USA, tel: 603-430-4433; Rent a Home International, 7200 34th Ave. NW, Seattle, WA 98117, USA, tel: 206-789-9377; VHR Worldwide, 235 Kensington Ave, Norwood, NJ 07648, USA, tel: 201-767-9393; Villas International, 605 Market St, Suite 510, San Francisco, CA 94105, USA, tel: 415-281-0910.

Self-catering accommodation

Guesthouses

Prices in smaller Bahamian guesthouses can be very favorable and sometimes the rooms are in attractive, traditional houses. While they offer only a modest degree of comfort, there is often a friendly atmosphere. The guesthouses on the Out Islands are not usually as grand as the splendid houses in Nassau. Meals other than breakfast are rarely provided.

A New Providence hotel

Hotel selection

The following selections for some of the most popular spots in the Bahamas are divided into three categories: **$$$** = expensive, **$$** = moderate, **$** = inexpensive.

New Providence

Nassau

$$$Villas on Silver Cay, Silver Cay. PO Box N-7797, tel: 328-1036, fax: 323-3202. Small but luxurious hotel consisting of 22 bungalows on the privately-owned island of Silver Cay. **$$$Graycliff**, West Hill Street, PO Box N-10246, tel: 322-2796, fax: 326-6110. Old building in Georgian colonial style. Formerly a popular meeting place for the rich and powerful. **$$British Colonial Beach Resort (Best Western),** Bay Street and Marlborough Street, PO Box N-7148, tel: 322-3301, fax: 322-2286. Impressive edifice built in 1922, over 300 rooms. **$El Greco Hotel**, corner of West Bay Street and Augusta Street, PO Box N-4187, tel: 325-1121, fax: 325-1124. Small hotel (25 rooms, 1 suite) in Spanish style, opposite Lighthouse Beach. **$The Little Orchard**, Village Road, PO Box N-1514, tel: 393-1297. Holiday flats and cottages in a pretty location near Montagu Beach. Supermarkets, restaurants and sports facilities within easy walking distance.

British Colonial Hotel

The Marriot Resort

Cable Beach

$$$Marriott Resort and Crystal Palace Casino, PO Box N-8306, tel: 327-6200, fax: 327-6459. Luxury resort with Casino, shows, restaurants and bars in this newly-renovated, 857-room hotel. The nocturnal haunt of many New Providence holidaymakers. **$$$Le Meridien Royal Bahamian Hotel**, PO Box N-10422, tel: 327-6400, fax: 327-6961. Elegant, medium-sized hotel with 145 rooms, 25 bungalows. Under French management. **$$$Forte Nassau Beach Hotel**, PO Box N-7756, tel: 327-7711, fax: 327-7615. Nicely furnished hotel with over 400 rooms. In the heart of Cable Beach. **$$$Radisson Cable Beach Hotel**, PO Box N-4914, tel: 327-6000, fax: 327-6987. Located on the golden sands of Cable Beach, this huge hotel with over 600 rooms has its own casino. The complex has several restaurants, swimming pool, golf course and clinic and watersports. Las Vegas-type atmosphere.

$$The Breezes Bahamas, PO Box N-3026, tel: 327-8231, fax: 327-6727. U-shaped hotel next to the Nassau Forte Beach. Several restaurants and bars, plus special program for children. **$$Days Inn Casuarinas**, PO Box N-4016, tel: 327-7921, fax: 327-8152. Hotel with distinctive management style; 77 rooms and 14 suites. A genuine alternative to the expensive 'grand hotel'. **$Orange Hill Beach Inn**, PO Box N-8583, tel: 327-7157. A small, family-run hotel offering a friendly holiday atmosphere. Only 32 rooms and situated away from the hustle and bustle.

The Atlantis Resort

Paradise Island

$$$Club Land d'Or, PO Box SS-6429, tel: 363-2400, fax: 363-3403. Hotel complex with 70 units and time-share occupancy. **$$$Club Med**, PO Box N-7137, tel: 363-2640, fax: 363-3496. Club village lies at the western end of the island. 400 rooms in three-story blocks next to the beach. **$$$Atlantis-Paradise Island Resort and Casino**, PO Box N-4777, tel: 363-3000, fax: 363-3724. Gigantic hotel complex with around 1,200 rooms. Own cinema, shows, restaurants and bars are major attractions. **$$$Ocean Club**, PO Box N-4777, tel: 363-2501, fax: 363 22501. Small but high-class hotel surrounded by fascinating French-style gardens. **$$$Radisson Grand Hotel**, PO Box SS-6307, tel: 363-2011, fax: 363-3193. High standard of accommodation with magnificent view of the Atlantic. **$$$Sunrise Beach Club and Villas,** PO Box SS-6519, tel: 363-2234, fax: 363-2308. Small, attractive apartment hotel, set in a tropical garden.

Other accommodation on New Providence

$$$South Ocean Golf and Beach Resort, SW Bay Road, PO Box N-8191, tel: 362-4391, fax: 362-4728. This 280-room hotel and resort has its own private beach, golf course swimming pool, diving facilities and restaurants in the southwest of the island. **$–$$Sivananda Yoga Retreat**, PO Box N-7550, tel: 363-2902, fax: 363-3783. The retreat offers meditation and two yoga classes a day plus meals. With space for up to 200 guests in dormitories, rooms or camping in the retreat's grounds.

Grand Bahama

Freeport

Bahamas Princess Resort and Casino, PO Box F-2623. With over 900 rooms, it is by far the biggest holiday complex on the island. It lies in the center of Freeport close to the International Bazaar. It has its own golf course, 12 tennis courts and a large casino. There are two sections to the complex: **$$Princess Country Club**, tel: 352-6721; and **$$$Princess Tower**, tel: 352-9661, fax (for both sections): 352-4485. **$$Xanadu Beach and Marina Resort**,

The Princess Tower

PO Box F-2438, tel: 352-6782/3, fax: 352-5799. Sometimes called the 'Pink Palace', the hotel was for years the home of the multimillionaire Howard Hughes. It lies adjacent to the beach and has over 139 comfortable rooms. **$Castaways Resort**, PO Box F-2629, tel: 352-6682, fax: 352-5087. A lively 130-room hotel near the International Bazaar. Facilities include swimmimg pool and restaurant. Bus service to Xanadu Beach. **$Sun Club Resort**, PO Box F-1808, tel: 352-3462, fax: 352-5785. Clean, well-managed hotel not far from the airport. Bus transfer to the beach. **$Running Mon Marina**, PO Box F-42663, tel: 352-6834, fax: 352-6835. Around 30 rooms with a nautical feel including eight deluxe captain's cabins.

Lucaya

$$$Lucayan Beach Resort and Casino, PO Box F-336, tel: 373-7777, fax: 373-6919. Large hotel with casino and entertainment program. **$$Clarion Atlantik Beach Resort**, PO Box F-531, tel: 373-1444, fax: 373-7481. Large, well-maintained hotel by the beach, under Swiss management. **$$Port Lucaya Resort and Yacht Club**, by Port Lucaya, tel: 373-6618, fax: 373-6652. Fairly new center with 160 rooms and its own marina. **$$Club Fortuna**, PO Box F-2398, tel: 373-4000, fax: 373-5555. Center, with all-inclusive facilities, about 3 miles (5km) from Lucaya Beach.

Lucaya hotel

Children are also entertained

Other accommodation on Grand Bahama

$$Deep Water Cay Club, tel: 359-4831, fax: 359-4831 or USA: PO Box 1145, Palm Beach, FL 33480, tel: (407)-684-3958. Small, remote center with 12 bungalows on the private cay at the extreme southeastern tip of Grand Bahama. Own airport runway. Popular with anglers.

Eleuthera

$$$Winding Bay Beach Resort, Rock Sound, PO Box EL93, tel: 334-4055. Very select center with 36 all-inclusive rooms in secluded beach huts. **$$Club Med Eleuthera**, Governor's Harbour, tel: 332-2270. 300-room club (all-inclusive) with full sporting and entertainment program for adults and children. **$$The Cove Eleuthera**, Gregory Town, tel: 335-5142, fax: 335-5338. Large and spacious, beautiful rooms in bungalows with terrace under the palm trees right on a small cove. By the beach. $**Hilton's Haven**, Tarpum Bay, tel: 334-4231, fax: 334-4125. Small, clean hotel (12 rooms) with adjoining restaurant under the inspirational management of 'Bahama Mama' Mary Hilton. **$Unique Village**, North Palmetto Point, PO Box 187, Governor's Harbour, tel: 332-1830, fax: 332-1838. Small hotel by the Atlantic coast. Friendly, relaxed atmosphere.

Harbour Island/Dunmore Town (Eleuthera)
$$Coral Sands Hotel, Dunmore Town, tel: 333-2320 or 2350, fax: 333-2368. This hotel is situated by the pink sandy beach. **$$Valentine's Yacht Club**, Dunmore Town, tel: 333-2142 or 2080, fax: 333-2135. A friendly holiday center for watersports enthusiasts, with its own marina.

(Many hotels in the north of Eleuthera suffered extensive damage during the 1992 hurricane. At time of going to print, some were still undergoing refurbishment.)

Bring your own yacht

Abacos Islands

Marsh Harbour
$$Abaco Towns by the Sea, PO Box 486, tel: 367-2227 or fax: USA (305) 359-3080. Pretty, spacious villas for up to 6 people, as well as one-room apartments. **$$Great Abaco Beach Hotel**, PO Box AB20511, tel: 367-2158, fax: 367-2819. Generously proportioned hotel rooms and holiday villas by the sea. Own marina with 180 berths. **$Conch Inn Yacht Club and Marina**, PO Box AB20469, tel: 367-4000, fax: 367-4004. Small, comfortable hotel with its own marina between the harbor and the town center. A popular meeting place for yachting enthusiasts and locals.

Treasure Cay
$$Treasure Cay Resort, c/o 2301 South Federal Highway, Fort Lauderdale, FL 33316, USA, tel: (305) 768-9530. (Hotel block not open at time of going to print.) Included in the facilities are several tennis courts, a golf course, own marina, 'Spinnaker' restaurant, bars and a magnificent beach.

Elbow Cay/Hope Town
$$Hope Town Hideaways, tel: 366-0224, fax: 366-0434. New and dream-like holiday villas (small boat included) with view of small harbour. Calm, friendly atmosphere. **$$Abaco Inn**, tel: 366-0133, fax: 366-0113. Rustic bungalows with sea view. Just outside Hope Town. **$$Hope Town Harbour Lodge**, tel: 366-0095, fax: 366-0286. Small, pretty hotel by Hope Town harbor. Popular rendezvous with mariners. **$$Sea Spray Resort and Villas**, White Sound, tel: 366-0065, fax: 366-0383. Simple, but spacious holiday homes at the southern tip of Elbow Cay. Own marina, friendly atmosphere.

Green Turtle Cay/New Plymouth
$$$Green Turtle Club, tel: 365-4271, fax: 365-4272. Outside New Plymouth. Tastefully furnished bungalows spread around the club's own marina. Popular with yachting fans. **$$Bluff House Club and Marina**, tel: 365-4247,

Most resorts offer snorkeling

A New Plymouth institution

George Town Harbour

Long Island beach

fax: 365-4248. Bungalows set high up on a hill above own marina. **$New Plymouth Club and Inn**, tel: 365-4161, fax: 365-4138. Historic guesthouse with friendly atmosphere. In center of the old town.

The Exumas

$$$The Bahama Club (Ritz-Carlton, open winter 1995) in the north of Great Exuma Island. The Exumas first 5-star resort with golf course and a 145-berth marina. **$$Club Peace and Plenty**, Queen's Highway, PO Box 29055, George Town, tel: 336-2551, fax: 336-2093. This pleasant hotel by the beach – once used to house slaves, the bar was the slaves' kitchen – plays an important role in George Town. The restaurant and bar are popular meeting places for the locals. Own beach on Stocking Island. **$$Coconut Cove**, PO Box EX29299, George Town, tel: 336-2659. A romantic and peaceful hideaway, right on the beach about 1 mile (1.5km) outside the town. **$$Peace and Plenty Beach Inn**, PO Box 29055, George Town, tel: 336-2550, fax: 336-2093. Quiet hotel by the beach, about 1 mile (1.5km) outside the town. **$$Staniel Cay Yacht Club**, Staniel Cay, tel: 355-2011, fax: 355-2044. Hotel with six bungalows is situated on the edge of the National Park and is very popular with amateur sailors.

Long Island

$$Stella Maris Resort Club, PO Box 105, tel: 338-2051or USA (305) 359-8236, fax: (305) 359-8238. A very friendly resort built in plantation style and under German management. Range of sports activities, diving and flying. Own marina. **$$Thompson Bay Inn**, PO Box 30123. Small hotel on Main Road in Thompson Bay. Bar makes a good meeting place. No phone and credit cards not accepted.

Cat Island

$$Fernandez Bay Village, 3 miles (5km) north of New Bight. Bookings through 1507 S. University Drive, Plantation, Florida 33324, USA, tel: (305) 474-4821, fax: (305) 474-4864. The best site on Cat Island, rustic-style bungalows by magnificent Fernandez Bay beach. Relaxed, friendly atmosphere. Own charter plane. **$$Hotel Greenwood Inn**, near Port Howe, tel/fax: 342-3053. Simply furnished rooms by long sandy beach. Swimming pool. **$Bridge Inn**, in New Bight, tel: 354-5013 or in Florida (305) 634-1014, fax: 354-5041. Simple village hotel, but quite lively in the evening. Five minutes from the beach. **$$Club Med Columbus Isle**, Cockburn Town, tel: 331-2458. Opened in 1992, this club brought new life to the island. Diving is the main focus for guests at the 270-room complex. **$$Riding Rock Inn**, Cockburn Town, tel: 359-